BANKING ON BLACK ENTERPRISE

BANKING ON BLACK ENTERPRISE

The Potential of Emerging Firms for Revitalizing Urban Economies

TIMOTHY BATES

Joint Center for Political and Economic Studies
Washington, DC

The Joint Center for Political and Economic Studies contributes to the national interest by helping black Americans participate fully and effectively in the political and economic life of our society. A nonpartisan, nonprofit institution founded in 1970, the Joint Center uses research and information dissemination to accomplish three objectives: to improve the socioeconomic status of black Americans; to increase their influence in the political and public policy arenas; and to facilitate the building of coalitions across racial lines.

Copyright 1993 by the Joint Center for Political and Economic Studies, Inc.

Joint Center for Political and Economic Studies
1090 Vermont Avenue, N.W., Suite 1100
Washington, D.C. 20005–4961

Library of Congress Cataloging-in-Publication Data

Bates, Timothy Mason.

Banking on Black enterprise : the potential of emerging firms for revitalizing urban economies / Timothy Bates.
p. cm.
Includes bibliographical references.
1. Minority business enterprises—United States.   2. Afro-American business enterprises.   3. Afro-Americans in business.
4. Urban policy—United States.   I. Joint Center for Political and Economic Studies (U.S.)   II. Title.
HD2346.U5B268   1992
338.6'42'08996073—dc20   92–73360 CIP

ISBN 0–941410–93–5 (cloth : alk. paper)
ISBN 0–941410–94–3 (pbk. : alk. paper)

FOREWORD

For some years now, the subject of minority business development has been largely ignored in Washington. Political candidates and seated policymakers often pass over in silence a topic that does not comfortably fit into majority-oriented campaigns. Timothy Bates' thorough analysis makes clear, however, that while existing policies on minority business assistance have often been badly mishandled, the potential returns from a fresh public investment in minority entrepreneurship are considerable.

The riots that destroyed whole swaths of southeast Los Angeles in the summer of 1992 should have sent a clear signal that patience is running out in our inner cities. Minority employers and minority employment there continue to weaken. Clearly, it is not good enough to plan for national economic growth while abandoning struggling African American urban communities to a downward spiral of vanishing jobs, skills, diplomas, and capital. We have seen how quickly violent crime and the illicit drug trade rush in to fill that vacuum.

In this volume, Bates marshals an army of hard evidence—well documented for the benefit of scholars and students—to show us where black-owned entrepreneurship has been going over the last few decades and what it means for the larger black community. Contrary to popular notions, he concludes, black-owned business is most alive and well not in the traditional enclave of mom-and-pop neighborhood retailing but in industries such as construction, wholesaling, and high-tech business services. The success of these "emerging" minority firms, he believes, offers the best hope for the inner-city economy.

Bates argues forcefully that government assistance to businesses can make an important difference to the well-being of inner-city residents, provided that it meets several conditions. First, it should be largely targeted toward minority-owned firms, for the figures show that minority owners are primarily the ones who hire minority workers. Assistance must also be carefully aimed at those firms with the potential to grow, not dissipated in loans to all takers. Bates takes pains in this book to analyze just which types of firms have that potential, and among other traits finds that they are the firms which reach outside the ghetto for their customer base. Finally, any policies must be accompanied by aggressive watchdog mechanisms to curb redlining and other discriminatory banking practices.

That may sound like a tall order, especially in a recessionary environment, but Bates argues that many of the pieces are already in place and only need to be strengthened or sincerely enforced.

One might expect that a thinker like Bates would have little to say in favor of the supply-siders' business remedy for the ghetto, the enterprise zone. But he argues that enterprise zones can be very helpful, so long as they mandate local hiring and are combined with public investment in the upgrading of infrastructure. Such an integrated, whole-community approach, in contrast to that which treats zones purely as "tax-havens," may represent an area where conservatives and liberals can find common ground.

The Joint Center has for many years been studying the most promising ways out of the economic impasse that continues to frustrate African Americans and other minorities. Timothy Bates' research, which we are very proud to have sponsored, has borne fruit in a realistic but also hopeful analysis. We confidently expect that this book will become part of the policy debate and hope its findings are listened to with a careful ear.

We wish to thank those at the Joint Center who have helped make this book possible: Milton Morris, vice president for research, for overseeing the work, together with Margaret Simms, director of research programs, Marc DeFrancis, senior editor, and Allison King, communications assistant. The author would like to acknowledge Alfred Nucci of the Census Bureau's Center for Economic Studies for his helpful assistance.

Our gratitude also goes to the Ford and Rockefeller foundations for funding the research that underlies this publication.

Eddie N. Williams
President
Joint Center for Political
and Economic Studies

TO BETH

CONTENTS

LIST OF TABLES

Tables in Appendices

About the Author

An economist with a national reputation in the field of minority business development, Timothy Bates has written numerous articles on the subject in the leading economic and policy journals. He has written or coauthored several books, including *The Political Economy of the Urban Ghetto* (1984), *Financing Black Economic Development* (1979), and *Black Capitalism: A Quantitative Analysis* (1973).

Bates has been called to testify before federal agencies several times for his expertise in minority entrepreneurship. He was an American Statistical Association research fellow in 1988, and in 1989 was a visiting scholar at the Joint Center for Political and Economic Studies.

He currently chairs the Urban Policy Analysis Program at the New School for Social Research in New York.

SUMMARY OF FINDINGS

Social scientists have repeatedly questioned the viability of the black business community. A recurring theme is the notion that black-owned businesses are heavily concentrated in several lines of small-scale service and retailing activity that hold minimal potential for growth. Indeed, the typical firm in the black business community has been the mom-and-pop food store, the beauty parlor, the barbershop. Such "traditional" lines of business, where most owners realize very low incomes, show definite signs of long-term decline.

Critics of minority business development programs have often assumed that emerging minority firms would be replicas of such common lines of business, but the evidence presented in this book largely refutes that notion. An emerging group of black entrepreneurs has been entering lines of business where minority representation has historically been minimal. This group is dominated by larger firms likely to serve a racially diverse clientele; increasingly, these firms sell to other businesses, including large corporations, as well as to the government.

Because my objective in writing this book was to analyze the role black-owned businesses can play in the economic development of urban minority communities, the emphasis here is on the most viable businesses—those relatively large-scale firms that are most likely to remain in operation and to create jobs. This profile, in fact, describes the emerging black business community. Unlike the traditional enterprises, where owners tend to have low levels of education and expertise and to invest little capital, among the emerging group the owners are likely to be college educated and to start their firms with relatively large financial investments. As a result of these differences, the emerging black firms prove to be larger in scale, have lower failure rates, and generate more jobs than their traditional counterparts.

Particularly rapid growth areas for this emerging group include wholesaling, general construction, and skill-intensive service industries, particularly finance and business services. The construction industry—certainly not a new line of black enterprise—is also evolving into an emerging line of business: growth in construction has been most rapid among the large-scale firms that do not rely primarily on minority clients. Opportunities offered by special corporate procurement and government minority business set-aside programs have also contributed heavily to the growth of these emerging entrepreneurs.

Black owners and whom they hire. This study clearly shows that in their hiring practices, white owners of small businesses continue to exclude minorities; black owners, by contrast, consistently hire minority workers. This pattern holds up regardless of the firms' location. White owners employ a predominantly—and often entirely—white work force even when their businesses are located in inner-city minority communities. By contrast, black-owned firms in the same communities utilize a labor force made up overwhelmingly of minority workers; only 3.2 percent of these firms employ a work force that is 50 percent or more white. Even outside minority neighborhoods, black owners continue to rely largely on minority workers, whereas most white-owned businesses have no minority employees at all.

In light of nonminority owners' aversion to employing blacks, an alternative strategy for opening up minority job opportunities is to promote the creation and expansion of businesses among the single group—black employers—that has already demonstrated its commitment to minority hiring. With that aim in mind, this book proceeds to examine the lingering barriers—lack of financial capital, limited access to markets, and redlining among them—that hinder black entrepreneurship, especially in the emerging lines of business where the potential for expanding minority employment and stimulating the ghetto economy is the strongest. These barriers can be categorized under three headings: problems of capitalization, narrowing access to government contracts, and barriers associated with the geography and poverty of the urban ghetto.

Three major barriers. The major constraint on the formation, growth, and diversification of black business in the 1980s has been inadequate capitalization. Black entrepreneurs' low holdings of personal wealth, combined with discriminatory treatment by commercial banks, have meant continuing obstacles. *Secondly*, court challenges to the constitutionality of minority business assistance programs threaten to reverse important gains made in broadening the range of markets served by black firms.

The *third* major constraint is geographically specific: inner-city black communities are increasingly being left out of the process of business development. Whether they are minority- or nonminority-owned, all firms suffer in the ghetto milieu, but the black business community suffers disproportionately. Among black owners, all three elements essential for business viability—talented entrepreneurs, financial capital, and access to markets—are threatened: the exodus of better educated blacks drains the pool of entrepreneurial talent, bank redlining blocks or limits loans, and weak local markets make it hard to thrive. All of this contributes to the very slow (and sometimes nonexistent) growth of black-owned businesses in minority communities. (See chapters four and five.)

Facing severely limited access to financial capital and weak internal markets, the ghetto firms that most commonly survive are far smaller, in sales and employment, than their counterparts outside the ghetto. Increasingly, the more highly educated and trained black entrepreneurs are going outside minority communities to seek opportunities. In fact, those black establishments that do remain in business in the ghetto are more likely to be headed by high school dropouts than by college educated owners.

Influence of black mayors and set-asides. Of the 28 large metropolitan areas examined in this study, 10 depended on central cities governed by black mayors. Evidence from case studies had already indicated that black mayors place a high priority on municipal contracting with minority-owned businesses. A comparative analysis of the 28 areas was conducted to see if black business performance, as a whole, has been aided somehow by the presence of black mayors. The examination found that it has in fact been so aided. Compared with black-owned firms elsewhere, those located in black-mayor areas are (1) more likely to be run by college graduates, (2) started up with much larger financial investments by their owners, (3) much larger in sales and employment levels, and (4) characterized by lower rates of business failure. Progress is most apparent among the younger, emerging lines of black-owned business.

Policy solutions. The calculus of profit maximization dictates that the choicest urban business locations today are in either the affluent outlying (largely nonminority) neighborhoods or the central business district. The most promising minority businesses, therefore, are increasingly likely to be located at some remove from urban minority communities. Present public policies, which too often assist the weakest minority firms or favor firms already locked within the ghetto, do little to reverse that trend.

By contrast, policies that would successfully assist the more capable, viable black-owned businesses would produce a derivative benefit: job creation for the residents of minority communities. Even though these more capable firms are locating outside the ghetto, the data in this study show that their geographic separation has not severed their employment link with black job seekers. In this vitally important sense, black enterprise does promote minority community economic development, quite irrespective of the employing firms' location.

The most prominent recent development in policy that threatens black business progress has been a judicial matter, specifically the U.S. Supreme Court's 1989 *Richmond* v. *Croson* decision declaring the minority business set-aside program in Richmond, Virginia, unconstitutional. Cities and states seeking to justify minority business preferential procurement programs must now be able to demonstrate that disparities exist between the minority business share of city (or state) contracts and the number of applicable minority firms willing and able to undertake such work. They must also demonstrate the presence of discriminatory barriers restricting the growth or performance of minority firms in the applicable fields. These two requirements can be met, in most cases, with readily available data sources. (Chapter seven discusses strategies cities and states can pursue to retain their procurement and set-aside programs in light of recent judicial constraints.)

Chapters three and five of this book show that commercial banks continue to redline black-owned businesses. This and other forms of lending discrimination serve to weaken black firms, in turn undercutting their ability to compete for government contracts. The practice of redlining is but one of a variety of barriers that local governments may cite to justify their minority business set-aside programs. Despite judicial challenges, therefore, it is possible that minority business assistance will continue to expand in the years ahead.

A final challenge is to bring inner-city minority communities into the economic development process. These communities need not be excluded from business growth if assistance programs can be reoriented, though admittedly that will be neither easy nor inexpensive. Key elements of a viable ghetto economic development strategy would require: (1) relying heavily on non-ghetto sources for both markets and financial capital, and (2) attracting the most capable entrepreneurs into the inner-city milieu. (See chapter seven.)

Entrepreneurial ability is highly correlated with both education and income levels: successful business operators tend to be above average in both categories. When government assistance accrues to better-off, better educated black business owners, the question invariably arises, "Why help those who are already successful?"

This objection can be addressed at two levels. First, the record shows that programs which target assistance to lower income, less educated entrepreneurs simply produce mass business failure. Second, the most capable entrepreneurs are also the ones likely to achieve the broader goal of economic development for the community, provided that the other ingredients of business success (capital and markets) are present. It is the viable firms, after all, that permit further business expansion and job creation.

Moreover, the presence of business success stories lures younger, better educated blacks into self-employment, and this further promotes economic development. Similarly, existing firms in less profitable lines of business are motivated—by the success story phenomenon—to reorient their operations toward products and services that offer greater profit potential; once again, economic development is promoted.

Most important for members of the ghetto community, if business successes increase in their area the resulting economic development will tend to reverse the drain of resources that exacerbates their poverty. Profitable operations build up additional capital and reinvestment, greater ownership of businesses by local residents strengthens the flow of income within (rather than leakage out of) the ghetto, and capable business people are retained in the community where their enterprises create income and jobs.

Seen in this context, the question, "Why help those who are successful?" really boils down to the question of whether the policy's goal is to promote economic development in minority communities.

1 INTRODUCTION

Overview: Why Black Business Ownership Matters

In an era when small businesses are creating a growing share of all net new jobs, access to employment in this sector is important to black economic well-being. In the dominant, nonminority-owned business community, however, the employment of minority workers is widespread only in blue-collar and service occupations. It is possible that minority hiring could improve as various antidiscrimination and other policies take effect. But affirmative action policies have never focused on access to jobs with small businesses, and equal employment opportunity laws and policies, by their very nature, are not designed to assist the black worker seeking employment in this milieu.

Consider, for example, the landmark Executive Order 11246, handed down in 1965, which established rules for nondiscrimination by federal contractors, subcontractors, and construction projects enjoying federal assistance. By this law, contractors with 50 or more employees and contracts of $50,000 or more are required to develop and submit affirmative action compliance programs with goals and timetables for the hiring and promotion of minorities. The key phrase here is "with 50 or more employees," which cuts out small enterprises. Moreover, in the watered-down, "race-neutral" form that they have begun to assume in the post-Reagan era, equal opportunity policies hold very little promise as a tool for widening job access for black workers. Yet one straightforward change in the small-business universe does have the demonstrated potential to turn this sector into a powerhouse of minority job creation: expanded minority ownership.

Poverty and unemployment among urban blacks have been worsening in recent years: wages among the least educated and skilled have been dropping and labor force participation declining. Within the black community, income inequality has been widening. At the top of the ladder, the percentage of black families with incomes above $50,000 (in 1990 constant dollars) is up substantially—from 8.3 percent in 1969 to 14.5 percent in 1990. During the same years, however, the proportion of black families with incomes below $10,000 also grew. Hardest hit have been the least educated and skilled members of the black work force; between 1969 and 1984, the real weekly earnings of black men who dropped out of high school fell by 32 percent, from $312 to $213.[1] If government relief agencies existed for the purpose of alleviating economic hardship, their assistance could have offset much of the suffering produced by falling real earnings and declining employment. In fact, low-income household heads generally receive no unemployment insurance benefits at all.[2]

In this tragic environment of growing ghetto poverty and declining government transfer payments, the only hope lies in increased employment opportunities. Blue-collar employment has been shrinking at the nation's largest corporations, just as the interrelated employment of less skilled workers has been shrinking in manufacturing generally. But in the small-business arena, net creation of low-skilled and blue-collar jobs has been pronounced.

Why does black ownership matter? Because the data clearly show that hiring practices among white owners of small businesses continue to exclude black workers, workers whom black owners nevertheless consistently hire. Even those white employers whose firms are physically located in inner-city minority communities hire a work force that is predominantly white; roughly a third of all such firms employ no minorities whatsoever. By contrast, 96 percent of black-owned firms operating in urban minority neighborhoods employ a labor force that is largely minority. Even outside minority neighborhoods, in areas where most white-owned businesses have no minority workers at all, black firms rely on these workers heavily. (These data are analyzed in chapter five.)

As pointed out earlier, affirmative action policies are of little help in combating the aversion of nonminority small-business owners to employing blacks. An alternative strategy for opening up jobs in this sector is to promote the creation and expansion of firms owned by the single group—black employers—that has already demonstrated its commitment to minority hiring. This book undertakes a close examination of the lingering barriers to black entrepreneurship—lack of financial capital, redlining, limited access to markets, and the like—in the hope that appropriate strategies for easing those barriers and strengthening black firm ownership can be devised.

The Crisis of Urban Black Poverty

The recent National Research Council study, *A Common Destiny: Blacks and American Society,* has documented the accentuated differences in economic status among blacks, "especially during the past 25 years."[3] Particularly among black men, earnings inequality has grown substantially since the 1960s. Between 1969 and 1984, the fraction of black men (aged 25-55) earning less than $10,000—an amount insufficient to maintain a family of four above the federal poverty threshold—grew from 25 percent to 40 percent (measured in 1984 constant dollars).[4] Rising unemployment and detachment from the labor force are partly responsible for these large earnings losses. According to *A Common Destiny,* "Between 1979 and 1985, the expected years of work for a white man fell from 39 to 36, but for a black man the change was from 36 to 29 years."[5]

Assistance for the working poor and the unemployed poor has become more meager over the years. A study by Sheldon Danzinger and Peter Gottschalk (1986) has found that in 1984 only 28 percent of unemployed household heads who had previously earned less than $5.50 per hour received unemployment benefits. Poor two-parent families with children qualify for little assistance other than food stamps. Family assistance benefits—virtually confined to single-parent families—have contracted even as black poverty has increased, their real value having fallen by at least 30 percent since 1973.[6]

The authors of *A Common Destiny* concluded that—barring changes in present conditions—prospects for blacks in the near future are bleak. Among the likely negative developments they foresee are a growing U.S. population of poor and undereducated citizens who will be disproportionately black and minority, a continuing division of social status within the black community, and further deterioration in the relative employment and earning status of black men.[7] What could be done to alter the "present conditions" and hence prevent these negative developments? According to the authors, "There are no satisfactory substitutes for a vigorous and expanding economy and an effective public school system to achieve an educated and employed work force."[8] Promoting a vigorous and expanding black business community is a complementary strategy.

This study of black business was initially motivated by my desire to identify the characteristics of businesses that have created jobs in ghetto areas and are capable of remaining in business. Particularly in the urban poverty ghetto, I sought to identify the kinds of firms most capable of contributing to economic development.

The Ghetto's Business Economy

Race and income are the chief defining characteristics of urban ghettos, but the geographic boundaries defined by race and income do not coincide. As we move out from the inner core of the typical racially segregated central city, the population thins out and its income and education levels rise. On the ghetto's outlying edges, the economic and social characteristics of the minority population are often indistinguishable from those of the surrounding white population. The mix of blue-collar and white-collar employment is similar, and unemployment rates are approximately equal. Neighborhood segregation is also less severe. The outlying edge of the ghetto differs greatly from the intensely poor and segregated cores of both the ghetto and the city. The racial ghetto and the poverty ghetto therefore do not coincide but, instead, overlap. (Throughout the remainder of this book, the term *ghetto* will be used to denote the overlapping area that is characterized both by poverty and by minority concentration.)

My initial search for black business success stories in the poverty ghettos of large urban areas was frustrated by the paucity of viable, job generating firms. Despite isolated instances in the ghetto of successful businesses, the overall pattern that emerged was something of a disaster. Highly educated black managers and professionals starting firms in major metropolitan regions are increasingly locating their businesses in nonminority areas, and they are catering to nonminority clients. By contrast, those firms that operate within the ghettos face weak internal markets and are severely redlined by commercial banks. All the key ingredients that promote business development—capable entrepreneurs, access to financial capital, access to markets—are in very short supply. Lacking these ingredients, the ghetto really has no prospect of generating the internal small-business development that could produce jobs and incomes for its residents.

Most fundamentally, the state of black-owned ghetto enterprises reflects the economic circumstances of their clientele. Weak internal markets reflect the obvious fact that poor people possess minimal purchasing power. It is true that the plentiful supply of cheap labor is an advantage to certain kinds of ghetto businesses such as building maintenance services, a labor intensive field in which urban black enterprises have steadily expanded. These firms draw heavily upon a low cost, blue-collar labor force to wash the windows, haul the trash, and perform other maintenance tasks. But in spite of the ghetto's cheap labor pool, most businesses cannot thrive there because of the weak market and the shortage of financial capital for investment. There are other obstacles as well: high insurance rates, high incidence of economic crime, decaying infrastructure, and poor public services—to name a few. In sum, the problems of markets and capital, in combination with these other ghetto attributes, severely limit the potential of a black business community that is oriented toward servicing a ghetto clientele.

Why Focus on Small Business?

Critics of small-business development strategies caution against relying too much on the small-business sector for employment gains.[9] The crux of their objections is concern that the jobs produced are lacking in quality and duration.[10] Although these concerns are often valid, the more relevant question is this: aren't jobs in small business—even though characterized by low wages, instability, and low fringe benefits—better than no jobs at all? Furthermore, the fact that wages, working conditions, and opportunities for advancement are on average less attractive in small business than elsewhere does not imply that employees in this sector are doomed, en masse, to a life of working poverty. Work in small business includes a variety of well-paid, skilled occupations—from auto mechanic to plumber to software supplier.

Structural changes in the urban economy are causing minority workers to rely ever more upon small-business employment. This trend has been caused in part by declining employment in manufacturing, offset by a rise in the service producing sector.[11] A growing body of evidence suggests that in recent years the small business sector has yielded the bulk of all new jobs. The highly publicized research of economist David Birch proclaims that firms employing fewer than 20 workers "have created about 88 percent of all net new jobs nationwide in the 1980s."[12] More credible studies have pegged the small-business share of all new jobs at 51 to 56 percent.[13] Whatever the precise figure on job generation, it is clear that urban black workers—particularly men in blue-collar occupations—are increasingly limited to employment (and underemployment) with small business.[14]

The decline of manufacturing jobs. On balance, the large enterprises that serve national and international markets have not added blue-collar employees to their payrolls in recent years. In large manufacturing firms today, growth in production depends less on the number of employees than on technical progress and improvements in physical capital per worker. A technologically advanced, capital-intensive production process now typifies large corporations. Their mode of production—and this applies equally to smaller firms operating on the technological frontier—stresses the combination of skilled labor and technically advanced equipment. Because firms in this sector are becoming more likely to grow by combining additional skilled white-collar workers with additional units of advanced equipment, output is often expanded even as jobs for less skilled blue-collar workers are cut back. The displaced workers naturally seek employment in small business because it is the only sector actively hiring people with blue-collar skIlls. For the same reasons, it is increasingly difficult for those seeking work for the first time to find high-wage employment in large corporations if they are not college educated. Those so affected, particularly young people and women, are therefore often more dependent on jobs with small businesses.

Until the 1970s, penetration into blue-collar manufacturing had been responsible for widespread income gains among less skilled workers, especially among black men. This traditional route to upward mobility has been lost. Worse yet, the massive losses in blue-collar manufacturing jobs over the past two decades have effectively reversed many of the black employment gains.[15] Between 1969 and 1984, the proportion of all employed black men who were working in manufacturing, mining, or construction dropped from 41.3 to 33.6 percent. Looking at occupational categories, the proportion of employed black men working as operatives dropped from 28.3 to 22.6 percent; young black workers have suffered disproportionately from this trend. Labor-intensive manufacturing has been especially hard hit. These job losses have been most noticeable throughout the Frost Belt, disproportionately hitting the older manufacturing states.

Regional trends in black income clearly reflect the impact of these job losses. Median black family income in the highly industrialized Midwest was $23,671 in 1970, which was 73.4 percent of the median white family income in that region. By 1987, however, the Midwest had been transformed from the *highest* median income region for blacks (in 1970) to the *lowest*. Black family income in 1987 had sunk to $16,755 (in constant dollars), which was only 52.1 percent of the comparable income for whites. High-wage jobs in manufacturing had been heavily displaced, and the only categories for black male workers registering substantial growth were service employment, unemployment, and labor force nonparticipation. The single line of service employment that grew most rapidly in the Midwest was also the least stable and offered the lowest wages: employment in restaurants and bars.[16]

Meanwhile, in many cities where manufacturing jobs losses have been pronounced, highly educated blacks have continued to gain managerial and professional employment. It is precisely in the older industrial cities, such as Chicago, Cleveland, and Pittsburgh, where the contrast between the haves and the have-nots is sharpening most rapidly.

Why Focus on Businesses Owned by Blacks?

Equal employment opportunity policies have traditionally been designed to improve the access black workers have to the higher-wage sectors of the economy—particularly government and big business. In the pre-1970s era, when these sectors were expanding their blue-collar ranks, this policy emphasis also benefited less-skilled black workers.[17] But in an era of declining blue-collar employment at large corporations, equal opportunity policies have become relevant primarily to the white-collar portion of the labor force, because it is here that big business continues to generate job opportunities.

Employment discrimination is certainly not permitted by law in the small-business sector, but it is not outlawed effectively. The structure of small-scale competitive industry usually makes litigation to enforce nondiscrimination employment prohibitively expensive. A further problem is the frequent inapplicability of affirmative action concepts: a goal of 20 percent minority employment does not fit the situation of a small business with two paid employees. Finally, even where the laws are applicable, enforcement agencies rarely pay attention to the practices of the multitude of tiny firms.

Largely unprotected by antidiscrimination safeguards, black workers competing for jobs in small business must contend with institutionalized practices that tend to undercut their chances of being hired. Small businesses large enough to utilize paid employees are overwhelmingly owned by nonminorities. Among the very small firms in this category, employees are most commonly either members of the owner's immediate family, relatives, or friends. In short, because employees are likely to belong to nonminority social networks that are family based, blacks are likely to be excluded.

A number of studies have found that young blacks and whites tend to use different job search techniques. While blacks tend to walk in and apply, whites are more often referred by friends or relatives.[18] A study by Henry Braddock and James McPartland (1987) found that the quality of employment blacks obtain correlates directly with the racial composition of their social networks. They found that blacks who attended racially mixed high schools were more likely to live in racially mixed neighborhoods and work in racially mixed job settings. Segregated networks lead to poor paying, more segregated jobs, they concluded, and "desegregated networks lead to better paying, less segregated work".[19]

This pattern of social networks helps explain why the racial composition of the work force employed by black small-business owners differs so profoundly from that employed by nonminority owners. Small firms tend to draw their employees from family-based networks. For essentially the same reasons, nonminority-owned firms primarily hire nonminority workers and black-owned firms employ a labor force consisting almost entirely of minority workers.

Recognizing the Potential of Emerging Black Businesses

Social scientists have repeatedly questioned the viability of the overall black business community, and they have often attacked government loan assistance and procurement programs as wasteful and ineffective.[20] A recurring theme is the notion that black-owned businesses are heavily concentrated in small-scale services and retailing, activities that hold little potential for growth. Most of these firms have no employees, annual sales below $25,000, and very high failure rates.[21]

In his influential early writings on black self-employment, economist Andrew Brimmer argued that the typical black-owned business lacked the technical, managerial, and marketing competence needed to compete successfully in the mainstream business world.[22] The state of black business in today's urban poverty ghetto provides little basis for refuting Brimmer's view of the ability of black enterprise to compete.

Looking beneath the aggregate statistics, however, one finds that the black business community falls into two very distinct groups. The first consists of the more numerous traditional lines of business, such as small-scale retailing and personal services. This group continues to be dominated by less educated owners whose firms bring in small earnings, and it shows definite signs of long-term decline. But there is also an emerging group of self-employed black entrepreneurs who are entering lines of businesses where minority presence has historically been scarce. These include wholesaling, business services, finance, manufacturing, general contracting, and professional services.

Critics of minority business development programs have often assumed that the black firms that continue to emerge would be replicas of the existing species—that the black business community would primarily yield more small retail and personal-service firms.[23] Evidence presented in this volume largely refutes that notion; the new and expanding black businesses do not conform with the stereotype of the past. The lines of black enterprise with the best prospects, however, are increasingly situated in nonminority locations. Among black-owned firms in such locations, the evidence (elaborated in chapter five) shows that more than half the owners starting firms have attended college, and that the businesses most likely to remain active are those (1) started by owners with four or more years of college, (2) having larger investments of financial capital, and (3) appealing to a racially diverse clientele.

It would be a mistake, therefore, to focus too narrowly on ghetto poverty areas in the effort to understand the contribution black business development may make to the overall economic well-being of minority communities. The growing, viable lines of black business—the ones that are most actively creating jobs—are disproportionately located not in the ghetto but in the central business districts and affluent outlying neighborhoods of large metropolitan areas. Moreover, the employment link between black-owned firms and the minority community is quite strong irrespective of where the firms themselves are located. As mentioned earlier, most white-owned small businesses in nonminority neighborhoods employ no minority workers whatsoever; by contrast, in 1982 fully 97 percent of black employers in these same areas utilized minority workers (and in most cases minorities made up over 75 percent of the labor force). In short, their geographic separation from ghetto areas has not severed the employment link between black-owned businesses and black job seekers.

Identifying the Barriers to Black Business

After the 1960s, the traditionally "backward" black business community started to diversify and expand in response to an influx of entrepreneurial talent and financial capital. Opportunities created by policies such as set-asides and preferential procurement programs have induced better educated younger blacks to create and expand firms in new lines of business including wholesaling, contracting, and skill-intensive services. Aggregate figures on black-owned businesses understate this progress because they fail to separate two divergent trends: absolute decline in many traditional lines of business and real progress in emerging fields.

This book identifies three major barriers to the progress of emerging black businesses. The most serious constraint on the formation, growth, and diversification of black business has been rooted in problems of capitalization. Taken together, lack of personal wealth holdings and discriminatory treatment by commercial banks have produced an enormous obstacle to existing as well as potential black entrepreneurs. Second, challenges to the constitutionality of minority business assistance programs now threaten to reverse many of the gains made in broadening black enterprises' markets. If minority business set-asides at the state and local levels are to survive, they will need to be reoriented in light of the judicial constraints imposed by the Supreme Court's 1989 *Richmond* v. *Croson* ruling.

A third major constraint on black business viability is geographically specific. Black communities in the inner city are being left out of the business development process. In the inner-city milieu, all three requirements of business viability—financial capital, markets, and talented entrepreneurs—are threatened: banks redline, local customers have little purchasing power, and better educated entrepreneurs are pulling out. It may yet be possible to reorient minority business assistance so that ghetto communities can enjoy business growth and investment, but doing so will be neither easy nor inexpensive.

A Better Direction for Public Policy

Discussions of policy options for assisting minority-owned businesses are sterile in the absence of clearly specified goals. Is the goal to promote black business ownership as an end in itself, or is black enterprise envisioned as a catalyst for the ghetto's economic development? Another question that must be answered at the outset if conflict is to be avoided concerns the target recipients: should they be the most "deprived" minorities who (for that reason) need the help most, or should they be those who have better prospects for success in self-employment? Typically, government assistance focuses on only one of the three essential elements of viability—either financial capital or markets. Some programs even perversely insist that the third element—entrepreneurial talent—be treated as grounds for *denying* financial or market assistance. The failure of such programs is well documented.[24]

Entrepreneurial ability is highly correlated with both education and income levels: successful business operators tend to be above average in both categories. The question that invariably arises when government assistance accrues to wealthier, better educated black entrepreneurs is "Why help those who are already successful?" This objection can be addressed at two levels. First, programs that target assistance to lower-income, less educated entrepreneurs simply produce mass business failure. Second, only the more capable entrepreneurs are likely to contribute to the larger goal of economic development, provided, of course, that the other ingredients of business success (capital and markets) are present. It is among these viable firms, after all, that further business expansion and job creation take place. The presence of business success stories lures younger, better educated blacks into self-employment, and this further promotes the goal of economic development. Finally, existing firms in less profitable lines of business become motivated—by the success story phenomenon—to reorient their operations toward products and markets that offer greater profit potential. Once again, economic development is promoted.

If business success is achieved on a wider scale in urban minority communities, the process of economic growth will tend to reverse the resource drains that exacerbate ghetto poverty. Profitable operations will create additional capital and attract reinvestment; the ownership of local businesses by local residents will strengthen flows of income within the ghetto; and the most capable business people will be more willing to remain in the minority community, where their own enterprises can create yet further income and jobs. In this context, the question "Why help those who are successful?" really boils down to the question of whether the policy goal is to promote minority communities' economic development.

Concluding Comments

My emphasis throughout this book has been to identify the most viable black-owned businesses—those large-scale firms that are most likely to remain in operation and to create jobs. This emphasis is dictated by my choice of policy objectives—enabling black-owned businesses to fulfill their potential as catalysts of economic development in minority communities. The policy discussions in chapter seven are similarly shaped by my premise that economic development is the appropriate objective for government efforts that seek to assist the black business community.

Current public programs (such as most enterprise zone efforts) often fail because their emphasis on ghetto locations means minority firms with the best potential are left out. During the 1980s, the successful black firms that were most capable of generating economic development increasingly chose not to locate in inner-city minority communities. Their calculus of profit maximization has shown them that the choicest urban business sites are either in affluent outlying (largely nonminority) areas or in the central business district. Present public policies have not reversed this geographical preference. Policies that would successfully assist the more capable businesses, on the other hand, would yield the derivative benefit of minority job creation. As noted before, geographic separation has not severed the employment link between black job seekers who live in the ghetto and black business located well outside the ghetto.

Critics of small-business assistance are right to point out that this sector of the economy offers lower wages and narrower room for advancement. Mere reliance upon small business to absorb the less educated and skilled members of the labor force cannot, by itself, be an effective long-run strategy for alleviating poverty and underemployment. Blacks remain overrepresented in the ranks of those lacking educational credentials and job specific skills.[25] The government's investment in basic education and job training must be strengthened so that young minority workers will have the skills they need to rise out of the lower depths of the job market.

The more traditional approach to improving black economic well-being has stressed programs for equal employment opportunity and affirmative action. Between 1964 and 1981, the federal government actively pursued such programs, bringing significant gains to blacks and other minorities: many individuals were freed thereby to move upward in government, educational institutions, the professions, and corporate enterprise. Today such programs are in a general state of decline. While the goals themselves still exist, compliance with them increasingly became voluntary in the 1980s. Moreover, recent Supreme Court rulings have narrowed the scope of equal opportunity laws, and "race neutral" policies appear to be preferred by the post-Reagan federal judiciary. Fighting for the retention of equal opportunity policies is certainly still worthwhile; continuing earnings disparities between whites and blacks with similar educational and work backgrounds indicate that discrimination in the labor market persists.

The equal opportunity strategy is based on the assumption that one's position and rewards are the results of individual ability and effort. It assumes that if the race is fair the swift will win. Unfortunately, a narrowly conceived, race-neutral equal opportunity agenda may well be exploited as a rationale for not attacking the fundamental causes of poverty and racial inequality. An expansion of opportunities for some people is quite consistent with further losses for most people. Indeed, the last two decades—an era of widening professional opportunities for minorities—have also been a time when the gap between the haves and the have-nots has been growing.

The present day's equal opportunity strategy is not enough. Ghettos, if they ever do cease to exist in the nation, will do so because their residents are fully employed at a living wage. Strategies that create jobs and enhance worker productivity, affecting small businesses as well as large and touching the lives of minority workers at all skill levels, could do much to move society in that direction.

2 TRADITIONAL AND EMERGING LINES OF BLACK ENTERPRISE

Traditionally, the typical firm in the black business community has been the mom and pop food store, the beauty parlor, the barbershop. These tiny firms have been concentrated in black neighborhoods and have served local clienteles. Breaking into larger scale lines of business has always been difficult for self-employed blacks due to barriers and constraints deeply rooted in American society. Although many of these constraints still linger, over the last few decades the black business community has begun to enter the business mainstream.

Critics of minority business development programs have often assumed that black business startups would simply mirror, with all their limitations, the traditional fields of black entrepreneurship. In fact, the lines of black enterprise that are growing today are not the small neighborhood establishments. Rather, they are the larger firms operating in industries where, historically, minority presence has been minimal. Many of the black entrepreneurs who run them have college degrees. Their mode of operation also sets them apart from traditional minority businesses—their mean annual sales volumes are far higher than sales among traditional firms, and they often have paid employees, serve a racially diverse clientele, and sell to other businesses, including large corporations and the government.

Because minority ownership within these growth industries has in the past been minimal, such lines of minority business are commonly (and throughout this book) referred to as "emerging" businesses. Emerging minority firms whose growth has been particularly rapid include the skill-intensive service industries: finance, business services, and various professional services. Even the construction industry, certainly not a new line of black enterprise, is nevertheless evolving into an emerging line of black business: growth in construction receipts has accrued to large-scale firms that do not rely primarily upon a minority clientele.[1] The growth of this and other emerging lines of black business has been heavily aided by corporate and government minority set-aside programs.

Recent studies indicate that all minority groups—Asians and Hispanics as well as blacks—prosper in self-employment in direct proportion to the degree that they are moving away from traditional fields like personal services.[2] Traditional black firms tend to be small in scale, have high failure rates, and generate few jobs; this is because their owners tend to have low levels of education and skill and to invest little capital in their ventures. By contrast, emerging black firms, started by better educated owners who invest more money in them than do traditional owners, are larger, fail less often, and generate more jobs.

In sum, success within today's black business community may be largely explained by these dual trends of traditional versus emerging firms. By increasing their investments of financial capital, education, and professional skill, black entrepreneurs over the past three decades have begun to move into emerging fields, where the chances for success are highest.

Traditional Lines of Black Enterprise in Historical Perspective

A long-term perspective on the development of black enterprise is vital for understanding why the trends in the traditional and emerging sectors have moved in such different directions. From its origins, the black business community has been shaped by limited access to credit, limited opportunities for education and training, and white stereotypes about the roles of minorities in society. In his landmark 1944 book, *An American Dilemma*, economist Gunnar Myrdal observed,

> The Negro businessman encounters greater difficulties than whites in securing credit. This is partially due to the marginal position of Negro business. It is also partly due to prejudicial opinions among whites concerning business ability and personal reliability of Negroes. In either case a vicious circle is in operation keeping Negro business down.

The role played by discrimination in shaping black business has been all-encompassing. Labor market discrimination has made it difficult for blacks to accumulate the minimal wealth required for initial investment in a new business. The dearth of black-owned construction companies in unionized urban areas was partially caused by the traditional practice of barring blacks from entering apprentice programs in the building trades.

Limited educational opportunities have, historically, handicapped black entrepreneurs in many lines of business. Until recently, even those who attended college were hemmed in by social attitudes about which occupations were appropriate for blacks. Between 1912 and 1938, 73 percent of black college graduates became either preachers or teachers.[3] A fortunate few were allowed into medicine, dentistry, and law, areas where they could serve an all-black clientele, but graduates were exceedingly rare in fields such as engineering, accounting, and general business. Such constraints produced a black business community consisting largely of very small firms concentrated in a few lines of business—beauty parlors, barber shops, restaurants, cleaning and pressing, shoe shine, mom and pop food stores.

More fundamentally, the traditional black business community was shaped by a specific time period—the 19th century—and a specific region: the South. The case of the skilled black artisan illustrates how profoundly discrimination has undermined and distorted the emergence of black entrepreneurship. At one time blacks dominated many of the South's skilled trades; as of the end of the Civil War, they accounted for an estimated 100,000 out of a total of 120,000 artisans in the Southern states.[4]   Rather than depending upon white labor, slavemasters typically relied upon their enslaved black workers who were trained in carpentry, blacksmithing, and other skilled trades. Mechanics working in bondage were often allowed to hire out on their own in return for a fixed sum of money or a percentage of their own earnings. Skilled white workers appealed to their government, demanding that blacks be restricted by law to menial jobs. The white workers' efforts largely failed, however, because the planter-dominated legislatures saw limitations on slave labor as a threat to the value of their property.

The circumstances of emancipation undermined the black artisan class. Their jobs no longer shielded by the slave-owners, these artisans now had to compete in a free, unprotected market while whites were protected by craft unions and Jim Crow institutions. South Carolina, for example, required after 1865 that blacks seeking work as artisans, mechanics, or shopkeepers purchase licenses—priced at 10 dollars annually—which whites were not required to buy.[5] Meanwhile, the craft unions effectively diminished the ranks of black artisans through the union's system of apprenticeship. This last tactic was most effective in the heavily unionized Northern cities.[6]

Since white entrepreneurs avoided trades that connoted servility, in certain fields blacks had virtually no competition. Personal service occupations were freely open to those of them who could obtain enough capital. In the antebellum South, blacks had a near monopoly as cooks, as well as on barbershops, beauty parlors, and cleaning and pressing establishments.[7] While low social status was in this sense an asset to most black entrepreneurs, it was a distinct handicap to the few who ventured into merchandising. By the mid-19th century, most Southern states had passed laws forbidding blacks from running firms in fields that required a knowledge of reading and writing, relegating them to occupations that society deemed "appropriate" with freed-slave status.

Little changed over the next century. In 1944, the first large-scale quantitative study of the black business community was undertaken. Joseph Pierce's survey of 3,866 black firms in 12 cities revealed an industry concentration reminiscent of the antebellum South.[8] Six lines of personal services and retailing dominated his sample of black firms: beauty parlors and barber shops, 1,005; eating places, 741; food stores, 293; cleaning and pressing, 288; shoe shine and repair, 183; funeral parlors, 126. When Pierce asked black businessmen to rank the most significant obstacles to entrepreneurship, they most frequently cited lack of capital.

Similar findings were arrived at by less comprehensive studies undertaken over the next 25 years: the black business community was consistently found to consist of small-scale operations concentrated in a few lines of activity that offered little potential for growth.[9] As late as the 1960s, the most common lines of business mirrored the black business community before the Civil War.

Easing the Historic Constraints

The barriers to black business progress described above— limited education, training, access to capital, and the rest—have eased substantially over the last 25 years. In the 1960s, government loans became widely available to actual and prospective black entrepreneurs. The commercial banks' tradition of minimal contact between lending departments and black customers eroded as the government introduced new guarantees against default. These guarantees induced thousands of banks to extend business loans to minorities. At the same time, college enrollment among black students grew dramatically in the 1960s and 1970s, especially in business-related fields.[10]

While increased loan availability typified minority business promotion in the 1960s, corporate and government targeting of procurement dollars and "set-asides" for minority firms did not become a major force until the late 1970s. Since then, large consumer products corporations have routinely earmarked procurement dollars to minority firms, advertised in minority-owned publications, and deposited funds in minority-owned banks.

Local governments have been widely using minority set-asides and preferential procurements throughout the 1980s, a trend that reflects the growing political power of blacks (and Hispanics) in many central cities. New York, Atlanta, Chicago, Los Angeles, Philadelphia, Detroit, New Orleans, Dallas, and Minneapolis are among the large cities that have shown "major support for minority business development activities."[11]   Indeed, chapter six of this volume documents one important manifestation of this local political power: the performance of black business in cities with presiding black mayors turns out to be noticeably better than that in other cities.

One consequence of this widened access to capital and education has been entry into previously unexplored new markets. While the traditional black business community was dominated by very small firms serving a ghetto clientele, the lure of market opportunity in recent years has induced entrepreneurs to create larger firms oriented toward corporate and government clienteles.

Owner Archetypes: Successful and Unsuccessful

In the universe of all self-employed individuals, the incidence of college attendance has risen steadily through time. This increase in educational attainment has been even more rapid among blacks than among nonminorities: between 1970 and 1980, census data show, college attendance rose among self-employed blacks by 120 percent, versus a 91.7 percent increase for their nonminority cohorts. The entrepreneurial importance of education is underlined by the fact that whereas among all self-employed blacks in 1980 only 28 percent had attended college, in the emerging minority field of finance, insurance, and real estate 66 percent attended college, the majority completing four-year degrees.[12]

That advanced levels of education and professional skill are pivotal to black entrepreneurial growth has been confirmed by other studies as well. In explaining the rising number of black-owned firms between 1972 and 1977, Handy and Swinton (1983) found that for a given metropolitan area (SMSA), growth could be most accurately predicted by three closely interrelated variables: (1) growth in the available pool of black professional and managerial manpower; (2) the initial level of black professional and managerial manpower; and (3) the general level of education among blacks living in the metropolitan area.

Building on what is known not only about educational attainment but about other traits and resources entrepreneurs enter business with, it is possible to sketch two composite portraits from the 1980s: one of the archetypal black business owner who succeeded, and one of the archetypal owner who failed.

The archetypal success: A college graduate, over age 35 but under 60, with an above average income, who enters business outside of such traditional areas as personal services, increasingly in such emerging fields as finance, insurance, and real estate. In terms of firm size (sales volume, total assets), the business is above average. Cash flow is strong relative to debt obligations. And the owner's initial investment of funds is relatively large; according to one recent study the size of this investment is the strongest predictor of success.[13]

The archetypal failure: A low-income individual who has not graduated from high school and enters business in a small-scale retail operation or in a service line of business that is not skill intensive. Financial investment is low and the firm size is small. The firm is often unable to achieve a scale sufficient to provide the entrepreneur with a decent income. With or without a loan, discontinuance is likely.

While those two profiles are accurate as model scenarios, success follows no guaranteed formulas. The world of small business is rife with model entrepreneurs whose businesses have gone belly-up. And more than a few high school dropouts have launched flourishing enterprises on a shoestring.

Trends in Industry Composition: 1960–1980

Although black firms today remain most heavily over-represented in personal services, the least profitable and the least capital-intensive industry, the diversification that began in earnest during the 1960s has continued, bringing a gradual but pervasive change to the black business landscape. Areas of rapid growth have become concentrated in such nontraditional fields as wholesaling and business services.

Although diversification had been well under way by 1972, national statistics at that time portrayed a black business community whose industry base was still quite narrow. In that year 63.7 percent of all black firms as measured by the *1972 Survey of Minority-Owned Business Enterprises* (1975) were concentrated in eight industry groups:

1.	Personal services	34,693	firms
2.	Miscellaneous retail	16,005	"
3.	Special trade contractors	15,616	"
4.	Eating & drinking places	14,346	"
5.	Food stores	11,887	"
6.	Business services	10,472	"
7.	Trucking & warehousing	9,938	"
8.	Gas stations	6,597	"

This 1972 ranking was unpromising, since few of these dominant industry groups would be growth areas in the 1970s. Retailing and personal services exhibited little growth in sales, while several retail lines, particularly gas stations and food stores, actually shrank both in number of firms and in aggregate sales and employment. Indeed, overall employment among black-owned firms declined in four of those eight industry groups between 1972 and

1977: only in business services did employment during this period enjoy rapid growth.

Looking at the scene 10 years later, we find that black firms were still most heavily overrepresented, relative to white-owned firms, in personal services, and most underrepresented in manufacturing. Table 2.1 shows how these disparate industry patterns in 1982 distinguished black-owned firms from firms owned by white males, which make up 72 percent of the small business universe and therefore represent the "norm" for standard comparisons. (These distributions were generated from the Census Bureau's 1982 CBO survey, described in Bates 1990b.)[14]

It is worth noting that personal services, which is the least capital-intensive industry group, offers both black and white owners the lowest remuneration.[15] Manufacturing, on the other hand, is the most capital-intensive, and has therefore been an area where self-employment has been difficult for blacks.

Table 2.1
Industry Distribution by Race of Owners: Nationwide Random Samples of Firms, 1982

	Black Firms	White Male Firms
Agriculture, forestry, mining	2.1%	5.4%
Construction	6.7	13.0
Manufacturing	2.1	9.0
Transportation, communications	11.3	8.3
Wholesale	1.7	2.9
Retail	27.3	21.8
Finance, insurance, real estate (FIRE)	3.7	7.2
Business services	5.5	5.6
Professional services	15.9	14.4
Personal services	13.2	3.3
All other services	10.6	9.0
Total*	100.0	100.0
(N=)	4,524	7,341

Source: CBO survey data (unpublished).

*Firms that did not report their industry affiliation (5.9 percent of the white male sample and 7.0 percent of the black sample) are excluded from this table.

Table 2.2 shows that 56.2 percent of the black firms sampled by the CBO reported 1982 annual sales below $25,000, as compared with 37.9 percent of white firms. Furthermore, 75.4 percent of these black firms had no paid employees. By contrast, white firms were more than three times as likely to be represented in the highest-sales category—$200,000-plus—as were black firms, only 4.8 percent of whom achieved that ranking.

In sum, despite nearly 20 years of convergence in industry concentration, blacks remain overrepresented in very-small-scale lines of business—in personal services and retailing—while white male firms are found disproportionately in the largest-scale and highest-earning lines.[16]

The shift toward skill-intensive firms. It is not valid to generalize about the nature of black enterprise solely on the basis of cross-sectional data. Since cross-sectional industry figures focus on one point in time, they invariably highlight the laggard position of self-employed blacks, even though most personal service and small-scale retail firms owned by nonminorities are marginal operations too. The firms that typify much of the nation's small-business sector are frequently struggling enterprises that bring their owners paltry returns; failure rates are quite high irrespec-

Table 2.2
Distribution of Firm Sales Levels by Owner Race, 1982

	Black Firms	White Firms
$5,000—$9,999	25.1%	14.9%
10,000—24,999	31.1	23.0
25,000—49,999	19.1	18.1
50,000—99,999	12.5	17.1
100,000—199,999	7.5	12.2
200,000—499,999	3.5	9.3
500,000 and up	1.3	5.4
Total	100.0	100.0
(N=)	4,883	7,807

Source: CBO survey data (unpublished).

tive of the owners' race. More insight may be gained into the changing nature of the black entrepreneurial world by examining comparable data on black firms at *different* points in time.

Such a review shows that although marginal operations are undoubtedly numerous within the black entrepreneurial community, a clear trend has emerged toward more skill-intensive lines of business. In 1960, owners of personal services accounted for nearly 30 percent of self-employed black entrepreneurs, while fewer than 10 percent ran skill-intensive enterprises such as those in professional services, business services, and finance, insurance, and real estate. By contrast, among the more recently established black-owned firms (in the CBO survey), namely those that began operations in the 1976-1982 period, only 10.3 percent were in personal services while 25 percent were in skill-intensive industries.

Even in certain broad industrial categories that are not generally labeled skill-intensive, such as construction, the distribution of sub-industries shows that minority firms have changed markedly. While special trade contractors in areas such as painting and carpentry have decreased in incidence, minority-owned general contracting and heavy construction firms have substantially increased. Similarly, the stagnation of retailing, including the steady decline of food stores, masks the fact that drug stores have been steadily expanding in incidence. These shifts reflect the movement toward more skill-intensive and capital-intensive lines of business within each of the broad industrial groupings (shown in table 2.3).

The overall industry shift between 1960 and 1980 is telling. In 1960, two lines of business—personal services and retailing—accounted for well over half of all minority enterprises, while smaller concentrations were working in construction and "other services." Collectively, these four most common fields—personal services, retail, construction, and "other services"—accounted at that time for 81.3 percent of self-employed minorities. Nevertheless, over the next two decades, *all* of the growth—as measured by the proportions of minority entrepreneurs in various lines of business—took place *outside* these four lines of minority enterprise. The most rapid growth took place in four other fields that, collectively, more than doubled their relative share of the black-entrepreneur pool: business services; wholesale; transportation and communication; and finance, insurance, and real estate.

The shift toward skill-intensive industries is reflected in figures on owners' earnings and education. Census data from public use samples indicate that in 1960, minority entrepreneurs (under age 65) had, on average, 7.6 years of education and mean self-employment earnings of $1,812; their earnings lagged behind those of minorities who worked as employees. By 1980, minority entrepreneurs under age 65 reported 11.5 years of education and mean earnings (from all sources) that *exceeded* those of minority employees by a wide margin—specifically, $16,105 for male entrepreneurs versus $11,235 for male employees.[17] All of

Table 2.3
Time Trends in Self-Employment: Percent in Various Industry Groups* of All Minorities Self-Employed, 1960 to 1980

	1960	1980	Percent Change Since 1960	Industry Growth Rate
Construction	16.7	16.5	-1.2	Stagnant
Manufacturing	4.1	6.0	46.3	Moderate
Transportation, communications, and utilities	3.9	6.0	53.8	Rapid
Wholesale	1.7	3.6	111.8	Rapid
Retail	25.4	25.4	0.0	Stagnant
Finance, insurance, and real estate	1.4	4.0	185.7	Rapid
Business services	2.4	6.6	175.0	Rapid
Repair services	5.2	6.9	32.7	Moderate
Personal services	28.9	14.7	-49.1	Declining
Other services	10.3	10.3	0.0	Stagnant
Total	100.0	100.0		

Source: Decennial Census of Population, public-use samples for 1960 and 1980.

*Excludes agriculture, doctors, and lawyers.

this suggests that the status of entrepreneurs within the black community as a whole has undergone profound changes. Even within the skill-intensive industries, the specialties blacks have moved into have changed considerably. Thirty years ago, blacks were concentrated in the fields of medicine, law, and insurance. Today, common lines of business include these fields as well as consulting firms, ad agencies, engineering services, accounting, employment agencies, computer software, and so forth. These findings reflect the trends toward diversity that are vitally important for comprehending the trajectory of black entrepreneurship.

Catch-up and mirror trends. By 1980, minority and nonminority entrepreneurs had begun to converge toward a similar distribution of industries, although minorities remained underrepresented in high-earning fields such as finance, insurance, and real estate. This convergence does not mean the two races were moving along the same track; the growth areas for minority self-employment have not been identical to those for nonminorities.

Two distinct patterns account for the evolving concentrations of minority businesses since 1960: one may be termed a *catch-up* pattern, and the other a *mirror* pattern. The catch-up phenomenon is clearest in the cases of manufacture and wholesaling. These have not been growing areas of self-employment for nonminorities; between 1960 and 1980, the share of nonminority owners in these two industries slid from 11.8 percent to 11.2 percent. In sharp contrast, the minority business incidence in these fields rose from 5.8 percent to 9.6 percent. Thus, minorities have been catching up in the sense that they have narrowed the gap between their own industry concentrations and those of nonminorlty entrepreneurs.

The second, simultaneous trend has been that of industries whose minority distribution has changed in a way that simply mirrors the change among nonminorities. In fields such as business services—up 175.0 percent for minorities and 169.6 percent for nonminorities—the two growth patterns reflect one another.

A combination of catch-up and mirror trends is evident in the finance, insurance, and real estate (FIRE) industry. First, minorities have mirrored the behavior of their non-minority counterparts in that both groups have been rapidly increasing their relative *numbers* in the FIRE fields. Secondly, while the proportion of all nonminority owners who were in the FIRE industry rose between 1960 and 1980 by 57.4 percent, the proportion among minorities rose even faster—by 185.7 percent (see table 2.3).

If prospects for black firms are to be accurately projected, and if the emerging trends already discussed are to be understood in depth, it will be necessary to review with some precision those traits that determine business success. The degree to which loan access, owners' education, and financial investment may make or break a business, and the extent to which these and other traits distinguish black entrepreneurs from white ones, are therefore considered in chapter three.

3 WHY BLACK FIRMS FAIL

W hile the trajectory of black businesses—moving toward larger firms in more diverse industries—is narrowing the gap in self-employment earnings between blacks and whites,[1] parity is not close at hand. The black business community, in its emerging as well as its traditional areas of enterprise, lags behind the nonminority community, with firms that tend to be smaller, less profitable, and more prone to failure. Among the CBO businesses analyzed in chapter two, mean 1982 sales were $138,030 for white firms but for black firms only $55,402.

By themselves, of course, those sales figures do not convey much useful information. To grasp the causes of the enduring racial inequalities in the success of small businesses, we need a broader analysis of firm and owner traits. This chapter therefore looks closely at the characteristics that distinguish weak, failure-prone firms from the larger, more growth-oriented lines of business. The relative importance of firm age, capitalization, and access to credit is explored, business survival rates over time are measured, and the differing traits of the people who own firms are identified in some detail.

The evidence suggests that highly educated owners, irrespective of race, invest larger amounts of financial capital into their small businesses and are more likely to create larger scale, lasting firms than are their poorly

educated peers, whose financial resources are less boun-
tiful. Given that pattern, the weaker posture of black
businesses is predictable. On average, black owners
possess less of the requisite financial equity and education
associated with business viability. And their access to debt
capital is more restricted than that enjoyed by nonminority
loan applicants. Smaller financial investments by black
owners at the point of business startup—less equity to
begin with as well as less access to debt—clearly lead to
the creation of black businesses that are smaller and have
lower chances of survival.

Yet the message of this chapter is not a pessimistic one.
The nature of the black business community is profoundly
different today from what it was 25 years ago. The size and
scope of the black business community have expanded;
industry diversity has flourished; highly educated entrepreneurs are the norm in many lines of business; bank
credit is more widely available. Overall, black emerging
businesses are progressing rapidly. But they must still
contend with a range of problems that plague small
business in general, as well as additional problems that
affect black firms disproportionately.

Defining Small Businesses

Too often, our perceptions of minority enterprises
and their status have been clouded by both a lack of
consistent definitions and a lack of comparable data on
nonminority firms.

Until 1987, comprehensive self-employment data were
available only on minorities and women, but not on
nonminority males.[2] While these sources did provide hard
evidence of the very small size of minority firms, they were
often misinterpreted as evidence of minority firms' distinct
nonviability[3] and led many to believe that only minority-
and women-owned businesses were dominated by tiny
firms. This unbalanced picture was finally corrected in
1987 when comprehensive information on self-employed
white males was published as part of the Census Bureau's

Characteristics of Business Owners (CBO) survey data. (See appendix A for details on the CBO data.) Table 2.2 in chapter two indicates that in 1982 large portions of white-owned firms as well reported annual sales of under $10,000.

Any insightful analysis of enterprise behavior must also begin with some clear definition of what a small business is. In government statistics, anyone filing a schedule C, form 1040 (sole proprietorship) federal income tax return is counted as a small business. This includes Avon ladies, college professors earning honoraria for occasional speeches, and millions of other Americans earning income through part-time self-employment.

That definition, accepted by many social scientists as well as by the government, flies in the face of the common conception of small business. Because of this definition, casual self-employment engaged in only when normal, full-time work is slack (such as a carpenter's moonlighting in home repair when building contracting is down) is later labeled as a business "discontinuance" when it is dropped; this occurs even though it may well be dropped because full-time employment has picked up again. Clearly, many business "failures" are not failures.[4]

There are several ways of separating "real" small businesses from casual ones, though none is perfect. The approach used throughout this study defines small businesses as those listed in the CBO data base for which (1) there was *some* investment of financial capital (greater than zero dollars) and (2) annual 1982 sales were at least $5,000.

Employers vs. nonemployers. Before proceeding with that definition, it is worthwhile to review what is revealed by using one popular alternative definition, defining meaningful businesses as *all firms with paid employees.*

Dividing the CBO data into employer and nonemployer groups is insightful. The firms thus described (listed in appendix B, table B.1) consist of 1,202 employers and 3,681 nonemployers among black firms, as well as 2,751 employers and 5,056 nonemployers among white male firms. Mean 1982 sales volumes for these CBO firms were:

Mean sales, 1982

Employers	Black firms	$138,030	■■■■■■■
	White male firms	$378,549	■■■■■■■■■■■■■■■■■■
Nonemployers	Black firms	$28,421	■■
	White male firms	$47,268	■■

For these same firms, the percentages falling into selected 1982 sales categories were:

		Employers	Nonemployers
Black Firms	Sales under $25,000	16.0	69.2
	Sales of $50,000-plus	62.6	12.4
White Firms	Sales under $25,000	7.2	54.7
	Sales of $50,000-plus	80.2	24.2

The 1,202 black employers identified in the CBO data employed 3,640 workers as of March 1982, and most of those employees worked for firms whose 1982 sales exceeded $100,000.

The employer-nonemployer distinction offers insight into who is most apt to possess the two traits—higher financial investment and better educated owners—that so consistently delineate stronger firms from those prone to failure. Relative to firms with no employees, employer firms are larger in scale, are run by more highly educated owners who make much larger financial investments in them, and are more likely to remain in business:

	Employers	Nonemployers
Percentage of owners with four-plus years of college	29.0%	23.0%
Total financial capital (mean)	$28,095	$11,929
Percent of firms still in business (1986)	82.0%	72.9%

That employer firms have better survival rates than nonemployers and that they are associated with more years of owner education should not be surprising. College graduates rarely enter such traditional fields as personal services, a field in which black-owned firms rarely utilize paid employees. Instead, highly educated owners invest in larger scale industries such as wholesaling where growth prospects are greater, owner remuneration is above average, and use of paid employees is the norm. In those rare instances where college graduates do enter into small-scale traditional lines of business, they are no more likely to establish lasting firms than high school dropouts.

Separating out businesses through this employer definition not only highlights the impact minority employers have on minority labor, but also highlights the correlations between owner education, owner investment, the use of employees, and firm survival. Nevertheless, while job creation and the racial makeup of the labor force are major concerns of this study, defining small businesses as employer firms alone would be too restrictive.

As noted earlier, more than 30 percent of the black firms without employees reported 1982 sales of $25,000 or more, and many of these small firms are operating in the emerging lines of business that have large potential for growth. Understanding the forces shaping these small firms will be just as important as understanding the forces shaping black firms with paid employees. The remainder of the study therefore assumes the broader sales and investment definition of small businesses.

Entrepreneurial Behavior That Shapes Small Businesses

Before examining the patterns of success among various kinds of firms, it would be useful to know whether potential entrepreneurs themselves start out on a level playing field, or even on the same playing field. Part of the uniqueness of the black entrepreneurial pool lies in the fact that the proportion of the black labor force pursuing self-employment is quite low, relative to whites. Why do blacks, as a whole, differ from other minorities and from whites in their likelihood of starting up enterprises?

The following discussion seeks to answer this, at least in part, by examining how entrepreneurs judge the costs and benefits of starting a business. It also looks at the influence of new and experienced owners' varying degrees of confidence and at the difference between taking ownership through a buyout and starting a firm from scratch.

As of 1976, among adult (over 21) members of the labor force, whites were more than three times as likely as blacks to be self-employed, according to national data.[5] At that time, the breakdown (including those under age 21) was as follows:

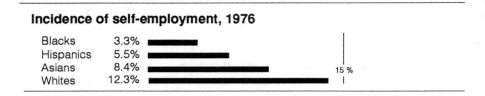

Incidence of self-employment, 1976

Blacks	3.3%	
Hispanics	5.5%	
Asians	8.4%	
Whites	12.3%	15 %

Peter Bearse (1984) has identified several traits that explain why the incidence of self-employment is higher for whites and Asians than for other minority groups, including higher educational attainment and greater wealth holdings. In wealth holdings, Bearse found that blacks lagged behind other groups.

Weighing opportunity costs. Another reason blacks enter business less frequently than Asians and Hispanics has to do with the perceived "opportunity costs" of engaging in small-business ownership. Particularly in high-wage areas of the country, self-employment will not be pursued unless it is sufficiently remunerative to compete with the wages available in the local labor markets. Highly educated and skilled people are particularly sensitive to such opportunity costs; they commonly have to sacrifice high-wage positions as employees in order to start small businesses as full-time ventures.

In an earlier study, the author found that Asians and Hispanics pay much less attention to the opportunity costs of enterprise than blacks do.[6] Small-business owners from these two ethnic backgrounds are much more likely than blacks to cling to self-employment in high-income metropolitan areas, even if the income from their businesses is low. In part, this reflects the barriers of language that restrict employment options for many Asian and Hispanic immigrants.

This is illustrated by recent trends in Asian-owned retail operations. Even though firm profitability is lower in retailing than in any other line of Asian-owned business, highly educated Asian immigrants entered the retail trade in very large numbers during the 1980s, crowding into the smaller-scale, less profitable lines such as food stores and restaurants. Educated Asians have been forced to enter such low-yielding enterprises by a combination of language barriers and financial capital constraints. For the same reasons, they have remained underrepresented, relative to nonminorities, in larger-scale retail lines such as new car dealerships and stores selling appliances and building materials. Predictably, mean 1982 sales for newer Asian-owned retail firms (formed between 1976 and 1982) lagged behind those of nonminority retail enterprises, $137,369 as compared with $175,509.[7]

These facts somewhat contradict the popular notion that Asian immigrants today, as a rule, are exceptionally successful entrepreneurs. Many of the low-yielding Asian businesses fail outright shortly after their creation. And even the "successful" operations do not tend to retain their founders. As English fluency improves and assets accumulate, the barriers that dictated self-employment in retailing ease. Once successful, the owners often leave retailing, opting for new work that permits them to make better use of their knowledge and skills and, generally, to earn more. The exception to this pattern is found in areas such as professional services, which offers Asian owners both the opportunity to utilize their professional skills and training and the possibility of high earnings.

Experience and entrepreneurial confidence. Quite irrespective of entrepreneurs' education and financial assets, the dynamics of their success depend heavily on a variety of entrepreneurial skills and talents. Boyan Jovanovic has pointed out something less obvious but equally important: not only do people differ in the level of skills they possess, they also differ in their ability to gauge them accurately.

Jovanovic's popular model of small-business development stresses the length of time an owner has been pursuing self-employment. People gradually learn about their managerial abilities as they run a business and observe how well they do.[8] As they learn more about their abilities, their entrepreneurial behavior itself changes: those whose self-assessments grow stronger tend to expand the size of their firms, while those whose self-assessments grow weaker tend to contract their businesses or dissolve them.

Jovanovic's model helps explain why younger businesses are so much more apt to fail than older ones. Younger firms behave more inconsistently than mature firms, in part because their owners are relatively less certain about their own managerial abilities. They may overestimate themselves and fail by overreaching, or underestimate themselves and stagnate. Because younger firms are usually smaller, this inconsistency characterizes smaller firms more commonly than larger ones.

When we subdivide the businesses reviewed in this study (from the CBO sample) into younger and older firms, their corresponding survival rates and sales figures confirm Jovanovic's characterization (see table B.2 in appendix B, where detailed statistics on these and other findings discussed in this chapter are illustrated through supplementary tables). Older firms here are defined as those which by 1986 were more than 10 years old (started before 1976) and younger firms as those which by then were from four to 10 years old (started during the 1976-1982 period). Regardless of the owners' race, younger firms consistently had lower annual sales in 1982 and were more likely to have discontinued[9] operations by late 1986, as the following figures show (figures for whites are limited to male owners):

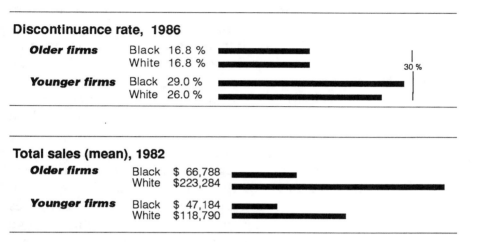

Discontinuance rate, 1986

Older firms	Black	16.8 %	
	White	16.8 %	30 %
Younger firms	Black	29.0 %	
	White	26.0 %	

Total sales (mean), 1982

Older firms	Black	$ 66,788
	White	$223,284
Younger firms	Black	$ 47,184
	White	$118,790

For both blacks and whites, annual sales ranged across greater extremes for the younger firms.[10] Their behavior is clearly less settled than that of older firms, consistent with the finding that their owners are in the process of learning how to run a business.

An important unanswered question, however, concerns the causes of the disparities between the mean sales and discontinuance rates of white male firms and those of black firms. As a group, the black firms are slightly younger than the white sample, but the difference is not substantial (see table B.2 in appendix B). So while the maturity of firms has a great deal to do with their sustainability and output, it does not go far toward explaining the gap in success rates that still separates black firms from white ones. In fact, black firms' lower financial capital investments account more than any other factor for their dramatically lower sales levels as compared to white firms and, among all younger firms, for black firms' higher rates of discontinuance.

Buyouts vs. newly formed businesses. If differences in firm maturity do not explain the racial disparity in sales volume, perhaps it can be explained by differences in the way new firms are obtained. Buyouts—businesses begun through the purchase of ongoing firms—may be contrasted with businesses started from scratch; buyouts may permit new owners to benefit from established managerial procedures and from some preexisting goodwill among clients.

Moreover, applying Jovanovic's thinking, a new owner who is unsure of his or her managerial abilities may reduce uncertainty by buying into a firm where the previous owner's practices are embodied in the operations. If such piggybacking on existing expertise succeeds, then the purchase of ongoing firms, other things being equal, should be associated with higher sales levels. The figures show, in fact, that buyouts generate much higher average sales than creating firms from scratch does, and they show that whites are slightly more likely than blacks to enter business via the buyout route: ongoing businesses accounted for 21.3 percent of the black CBO firms and 24.0 percent of the white firms.

Yet the huge disparity in sales that marks off black firms from white firms remains largely unexplained. The differences in firm age and frequency of buyouts, just discussed, could only be contributing in some small degree toward this disparity. It is noteworthy that the disparity widens among older black firms; this suggests that the higher incidence of *traditional* lines of business among black-owned firms is a contributing cause. While the mean annual sales of younger black firms were only 39.7 percent of white mean sales for younger black firms, among older black firms they were even weaker: 29.9 percent.

All of this suggests that entrepreneurial experience in and of itself cannot be assumed to be the deciding factor in explaining the weaker status of the black business community. Once more this points to the pivotal role played by the *nature* of emerging businesses and the importance of the shift away from traditional black enterprises.

Explaining Black-White Differences in Business Size and Survival

The firms that are most likely to remain in business tend to be the larger-scale operations. Indeed, a major finding of this study is that stronger business startups have greater access to financial capital; the better capitalized operations, in turn, become larger in scale.

My investigation into the determinants of small-business viability has been guided by the findings of previous studies that have linked specific owner and enterprise traits to the likelihood of business discontinuance and survival. These traits fall under five headings.

First, whether measured by sales, number of employees, or total assets, it is the *larger-scale* firms that are most likely to survive.[11] Second, chances of remaining in business become stronger as firms grow *older;* as a rule firms are most likely to discontinue operations during their first few years.[12] Third, the owners most likely to establish lasting firms are those having *four or more years of college.*[13] Fourth, the owners most likely to survive also invest substantial amounts of *financial capital* into their businesses.[14] A fifth trait, though less influential than the first four, is that of firms purchased in *buyouts*; they are more likely to survive than those started from scratch.[15] In the following pages we explore the relative influence of these five broad traits in assuring business startups their best chances of success. It turns out that the greatest single disparity between the samples of young white and black businesses lies in the two groups' financial capital structures. Whites consistently command much more financial capital than black business owners at the point of business entry: differentials are widest for debt capital. The debt factor in turn is linked to other startup traits, of course, since firms that can leverage larger seed loans from commercial banks are likely to be larger enterprises whose owners have strong resumés.

Firm size and firm age. That smaller firms, whether owned by blacks or whites, are consistently less likely to survive than larger firms is evident from the figures in table 3.1. Likewise, the table shows that younger firms are less likely to survive than older ones, and that this also holds true equally for blacks and whites and at every level of sales.

The pattern of firm survival is most readily apparent when one looks at the extremes of firm age and size. Among black firms, the percentage still in business in 1986 was 58.5 for young firms with sales under $10,000, but jumped to 86.7 for old firms with sales above $100,000. The same contrast holds for white male firms, which jump from 62.7 percent to 88.7 percent for those two sales/age categories. Another—and even more dramatic—way to

Table 3.1
Percentage of Firms Still in Business in 1986, by Sales Levels and Firm Age Group

	Black Firms			White Male Firms		
	Young[a] firms	Old[b] firms	All firms	Young firms	Old firms	All firms
$5,000—$9,999	58.5	78.9	65.7	62.7	70.0	64.9
10,000—24,999	67.4	82.0	73.0	68.4	78.1	72.1
25,000—49,999	72.8	85.6	78.7	75.7	84.8	79.6
50,000—99,999	82.7	85.1	83.8	81.0	84.9	82.8
100,000 and up	83.5	86.7	85.2	83.3	88.7	86.2
All sales levels	71.0	83.2	75.1	74.0	83.2	78.0

Source: CBO data on firms that were in business during 1982 (unpublished data).

[a] Young firms defined as those formed between 1976 and 1982.
[b] Old firms defined as those formed before 1976.

Note: Firms have been excluded from this table (and from the remainder of this chapter) if (1) their 1982 total sales were under $5,000, or (2) no financial capital was initially invested in the firm.

grasp these differences is to look at business discontinuance, which for both races was *more than three times as
likely* for the young, below-$10,000 group as for the old,
$100,000-plus group (table 3.1).

Note too that overall survival rates for black and white
firms, aggregated from all sales levels, are identical—at
83.2 percent—when one considers only the older businesses. And even among young firms, considering only
those with $50,000 or more in sales, the black firms have
a slightly higher survival rate (83.0 percent versus 82.3
percent) than corresponding white firms. In other words,
when enterprises are sufficiently large and sufficiently
mature, race plays no discernible role in longevity. Black
businesses lag consistently behind white ones in survival
rates only among young firms with annual sales below
$50,000 (table 3.1).

The greater prevalence of very small businesses among
black owners deserves some attention. Among all the
young businesses, 61.8 percent of the white male firms had
1982 total sales below $50,000. But even this high
incidence is vastly overshadowed by the incidence among
black firms of 78.3 percent. The abundance of small black
firms is partly rooted in the restricted amount of capital
available to them as compared with white owners,
limitations that work against the generation of higher sales
volumes. Comparative figures on the relative sales and
investment resources of young black and white firms
(table B.2, appendix B) indicate the following:

	Young Black Firms	Young White Male Firms
1982 Sales (mean)	$47,184	$118,790
Total Financial Investment (mean)	$19,066	$ 44,552
Owners with four or more years of college	28.5%	35.3%

In chapter two we found that the rising frequency among black firms of large-scale businesses reflects the rising incidence of highly educated black entrepreneurs entering nontraditional fields. Yet a countervailing factor that continues to depress the size of black businesses is the paucity of financial capital available for business investment. Traditionally, personal wealth holdings are a major source of capital for small business creation and expansion, and it is here that black entrepreneurs suffer their most crippling financial disadvantage. Understanding this disparity is essential for understanding the broad patterns of black business development, so the issue receives its own discussion next.

Personal wealth: black and white. A study of nationwide wealth holdings in 1967 showed that, on average, black families had less than one-fifth the wealth accumulation of white families.[16] Figures for 1984 show that this enormous gulf has not been narrowed.

The forms in which wealth were held also differed dramatically, according to the 1967 study. Equity—in homes, cars, and trucks—accounted then for 64.4 percent of aggregate black wealth but only 37.4 percent of white wealth; conversely, financial assets, the form most readily available for business investment purposes, accounted for only 10.2 percent of holdings among blacks but 30.1 percent among whites. Finally, equity in small businesses accounted for 5.7 percent of wealth holdings among blacks but among whites 9.4 percent.

Looking at the value of those holdings once again makes clear the size of the disparity. Even if we exclude blacks in lower income brackets and focus on those earning over $20,000 annually in 1967, we find that their average wealth holdings were $30,195 per household, roughly 30 percent of the holdings reported by corresponding whites ($101,009). Overall, white households not only held on average five times as much wealth as blacks, they also held well over twice as much of that wealth in the most usable form, namely as business equity and financial assets (39.5

percent versus 15.9 percent for blacks). In sum, the average white household in 1967 held more than 12 times as much of this readily investable personal wealth as the average black household.

More recent data on family wealth holdings in 1984 indicate that this inequality still prevails. Black households in that year had a median net worth of $3,397, versus $39,135 for white households: for every dollar of wealth in the median white family, the median black family had nine cents.[17] While only 8.6 percent of white households had zero or negative net worth, 31 percent of black households held absolutely no wealth whatsoever.[18]

In 1984, small business equity was most likely to be held by black households whose incomes exceeded $24,000; namely by 3.5 percent of those in the upper-middle income bracket ($24,000 – $48,000) and by 14.0 percent of those in the high-income bracket. For white households, the fraction owning this kind of equity was 11.0 percent in the upper-middle bracket and 21.5 percent in the high bracket. The greatest disparity in business equity holdings, however, derived from the fact that higher-income households are much more numerous among whites than blacks.

Disparities in personal wealth holdings therefore continue to handicap black business startups. In the 1980s, just as in the 1880s, black business creation has been heavily concentrated in industries where formation has required relatively little financial capital. Lacking assets—and therefore lacking borrowing capacities—black entrepreneurs remain ill-equipped to cope with economic adversities and to exploit economic opportunities.

Owner Traits That Most Affect Firm Sales

Given the clear importance a firm's size has for its success, it is useful to know which factors most forcefully determine whether a young business will survive and grow to a viable size. Yet measuring the effect of these influences can be difficult: they are inextricably linked to one another and they operate simultaneously. To disentangle these influences and measure their effect on such important outcomes as sales levels and business survival, in this section we employ a regression analysis that weighs each factor separately.

The analysis shows that of all the owner traits under consideration—the owner's education, entrepreneurial experience, own contribution of labor, et cetera—what most decisively accounts for the laggard performance of black firms is the investment of financial capital. This conclusion is accompanied by the finding that better educated owners are the ones investing larger amounts of financial capital in their businesses.

Owner's experience and owner's labor. In addition to such previously discussed traits as the firm's age and the owner's educational background, two other traits appear at first glance to be linked to firm viability. First, the owner's own labor—working full-time as opposed to part-time in his or her own small business—is expected to help in establishing larger scale, more successful ventures. The quantity of owner labor input is somewhat higher for whites, as these figures show:

Hours worked per week in own firm (average), 1982

Black owners	41.0
White male owners	45.8

Secondly, white owners had somewhat more managerial experience than blacks on the date when they entered self-employment:

Mean years of managerial experience, 1982

Black owners	3.7
White owners	5.6

Adding these two aspects of owner background into the list of factors covered so far, we now have five owner traits whose relative importance must be discerned. Are the lower sales levels that typify young black firms best explained by their owners' (1) smaller initial financial investments? (2) smaller number of hours put into their firms each week? (3) lesser amount of managerial experience? (4) generally lower levels of education? or (5) slightly lower likelihood of obtaining the firm through a buyout? (Buyouts accounted for 23.4 percent of the young black firms but 24.4 percent of young white businesses.)

To find out which of these may be the greatest cause of black firms' weaker performance, an econometric analysis based on multiple linear regression is used. This technique allows us to weigh separately a multiplicity of simultaneous factors in order to identify what weight each has—in this case, what weight each has in determining the size of a firm's sales. (No other statistical technique would permit the significance of a variety of factors to be weighed at one time.)

When the five owner traits listed above (as well as others) are considered simultaneously, it is found that the lagging sales of the young black-owned businesses are most decisively explained by the gap in financial investment.

The findings also indicate that the better educated owners investing larger sums in their businesses are the ones likely to establish firms with higher sales volumes. Other owner traits statistically linked to higher sales volumes are being in the 35–55 age bracket and working longer hours in one's business. (See table B.3 for detailed findings from this analysis.)[19]

The primary importance of financial investment is doubly confirmed by a further set of analyses. Two different econometric techniques—a multiple regression analysis and a multiple discriminant analysis—were employed to examine a pair of closely related dependent variables: firm size and the likelihood of firm survival. These differing techniques produced highly consistent findings, which may therefore be judged "robust" or reliable: that the size of an owner's financial investment is the most powerful single determinant of both the size and the likely survival of a small business.

If the financial investment made in a new business is so critical to its success, certainly the access to loans that entrepreneurs have ranks closely in importance.

Traits That Determine Access to Credit

In recent decades, black firms' access to credit has expanded. Relative to the situation in 1944 that Pierce described (see chapter two), circumstances have improved greatly; the fact that more than 25 percent of the black businesses that began operations between 1976 and 1982 received commercial bank loans is noteworthy. But credit access is certainly not approaching parity with white businesses. Black college graduates are least disadvantaged relative to white business owners, but black firms as a group are still less likely to get loans, and the loans that are extended are much smaller than those accruing to their white counterparts.

What are the underlying causes of this lingering disparity? Do blacks generally get smaller loans because their educational attainments, on average, lag behind those of white borrowers? Or is it their relative lack of owner equity that reduces loan size? Alternatively, perhaps black borrowers are restricted to smaller loans as a penalty for being black—?

To answer this, it is necessary to lay out the various forces at work and measure their separate influence through regression analysis. The following pages do this, and their conclusion is both simple and disturbing: statistically, blacks have been getting smaller bank loans than whites who possess identical traits as far as age, educational background, and possession of equity capital.

Debt vs. equity. When starting up a business, an entrepreneur's financial investment consists of two kinds of capital: debt capital, including both short- and long-term indebtedness, and equity, which measures the net worth of the small business under consideration, including the cash value of nonfinancial tangible assets (such as equipment and tools) that the owner has contributed to the firm. For the 1982 CBO samples of young firms (table B.2), the mean values for debt and equity capital were as follows (figures for whites limited to male owners):

Mean debt and equity capital, young firms

Equity	Black	$9,054
	White	$20,402
Debt	Black	$10,012
	White	$24,150
Total	Black	$19,066
	White	$44,552

As the figures show, the total financial investment at startup among white males was, on average, nearly two and a half times that among blacks.

The consequences of this huge disparity are profoundly important for explaining the generally laggard performance of black enterprise. The disparity is strongest in the case of debt, with the mean debt of black firms amounting to only 41.5 percent of the $24,150 figure for white businesses. (See table B.4 for details on the startup capital structure of young black and white male firms).

Commercial banks were the main source of debt capital, exceeding by far the combined total of debt extended to these firms by all other sources. Yet black bank borrowers reported mean debt inputs of $25,704, versus $55,803 for white firms (see table B.4; median values for debt reveal gaps of similar relative magnitudes). A racial disparity also persists in the proportion of firms obtaining bank loans, though it is much less severe than the disparity in amounts loaned: of the 4,429 young firms owned by white males (described in table B.2), more than 32 percent received bank loans, while the corresponding figure for blacks was 25.2 percent.

The importance of bank loans cannot be underestimated. For all of the firm samples—black and white—bank loan recipients began business with substantially larger amounts of both total financial capital and debt capital than firms not receiving bank loans began with. Among black firms, the mean financial investment was nearly five times larger for bank borrowers ($36,530) than it was for nonborrowers as a whole ($7,660).

Debt and equity are complements at the point of business startup. Among the white bank loan recipients, for example, the simple correlation between debt and equity was very high (+.62). One possible explanation for the differences in loan amounts obtained by blacks and whites may be that they reflect differing endowments of both human and financial capital. After all, blacks possess less equity capital than whites, on average; fewer black owners are college graduates; and white owners have more managerial experience. Banks are naturally willing to lend larger amounts to stronger borrowers, and white owners are more apt to have the traits, such as greater equity capital, that banks reward when they determine loan size. If differing loan amounts turned out to be based purely on these differing resumes, the disparities might be explained as a normal outcome of the process by which banks evaluate loans.

But the analysis does not show this. Rather, it shows that for each dollar of equity put in, banks provide the white business borrower with $1.83 in debt capital, all other things being equal, while providing the black business borrower with only $1.16. This finding, that banks treat white and black loan recipients differently even when their qualifications do not differ, emerged after determining the relative influence several factors had on the size of loans used to finance startups. The analysis, based on multiple regression equations, identified statistical linkages between the debt levels of bank borrowers and these types of owner traits: (1) the amount of equity capital invested, (2) the owner's educational background, and (3) demographic characteristics. In the end, the owner's race proved to be a significant factor in determining loan amount. (The applicable regression equations appear in the appendix; see table B.5).

Owner education and access to credit. While an owner's equity is the single most important determinant of bank loan size, his or her educational background ranks second. Among loan recipients, incremental loan amounts associated with having four or more years of college are $27,111 for black borrowers and $28,553 for white borrowers. College graduates face less discrimination from banks than do less educated black entrepreneurs. Among the owners of young black firms, 28.5 percent had attended four or more years of college (table B.2). These are the same owners that make up most of the emerging business subset of black enterprise, and they are the owners who have the greatest access to commercial bank loans.

The generally smaller loans to which black borrowers have access serve to restrict the size and scope of the firms they can create. This in turn leads to a greater hazard of business failure) The evidence discussed below demonstrates that size of financial investment is the single strongest determinant of business discontinuance: firms formed with minimal financial capital are commonly very small and they are the ones most likely to discontinue operations. Further evidence (chapter five) indicates that restricted access to credit is heavily rooted in the commercial bank practice of redlining firms that operate in urban minority communities.

Traits That Determine Business Longevity

Based on our earlier discussions of the traits that distinguish viable businesses generally, one should expect young black firms to lag behind young nonminority firms if they are deficient in those success traits. Specifically, the most successful black firms should be those that are

(1) older, established firms, (2) started with larger financial investments (including debt), and (3) obtained as buyouts rather than new businesses. One should further expect those firms to do well whose owners are (4) highly educated, (5) work full-time in the business, and (6) have greater managerial experience prior to self-employment.

This section reports on the findings of discriminant analyses designed to rank the relative significance of these determinants of black firms' survival. The results confirm most of the expected patterns, with financial investment looming largest in influence. Nonetheless, owners' education matters less than expected, while managerial experience has no clear-cut impact. And the buyout of ongoing businesses turns out to link more closely with discontinuances than with firm success.

Methodology. Discriminant analysis is a statistical method used to distinguish between two groups by discovering which of their shared traits most clearly set them apart. Upon mathematical analysis, the technique yields a "weight" (coefficient) for each of the traits (variables) being measured. Variables that turn out to have the largest weights will be those that best differentiate one group from the other. By distinguishing active, surviving black businesses from discontinued ones in this way, we obtain a better understanding of the root causes of black firms' success.

The CBO data base describes firms that were operating during 1982. In the discriminant analysis, a firm is defined as viable if it was still operating in late 1986. Businesses that were still operating are considered *active* firms; those that had closed down are considered *discontinued*.

Note too that discontinuance statistics apply to businesses rather than owners. Thus, a black-owned retail operation that was sold to an Asian is counted as an active firm as long as it was still being operated in late 1986. Mere departure of an owner is not equated with business discontinuance in cases where the firm continues to operate. Among the active and discontinued subsets of the black-owned young businesses, mean statistics on firm size and financial capital reveal major differences:

1982 total sales		
Active firms	$53,047	
Discontinued firms	$34,000	
Startup capital		
Active firms	$21,233	
Discontinued firms	$14,190	

The discontinued firms are clearly the smaller operations that began business with smaller financial investment. Summary statistics such as these are illuminating, but their limitation is their inability to rank, simultaneously, the relative significance of many variables. That is the task of discriminant analysis.

Distinguishing among the factors at play. The explanatory variables measured in this analysis include two firm traits—year of business startup and buyout of ongoing firms—as well as numerous owner traits describing education and experience, financial investment, and demographic traits. (These variables are defined in detail in appendix B.)

The traits hypothesized to be the dominant causes of firm viability have already been discussed. By way of summary, they are higher levels of education, more hours of the owner's labor, larger financial investment, and more years of managerial experience. Owners at both ends of the age distribution—particularly those over age 55—are expected to be less likely to remain in business. One previous study by the author indicated that owners in their late 40s were most likely to operate successful businesses.[20]

Highly leveraged firms are also expected to be more successful, due in part to the limited access to debt that bars many weaker firms from utilizing borrowed capital. "Leverage" is, by definition, the ratio of owner debt to equity; a higher ratio indicates greater borrowing.

Regarding firm traits, the youngest firms are hypothesized to be the least viable, while ongoing firms are assumed to be more viable than those started from scratch.

This is what the discriminant analysis reveals: listed in relative importance, the owner traits most directly associated with firm longevity are: (1) financial investment, (2) owner's age, (3) leverage, (4) hours of owner's labor invested, (5) educational background, and (6) albeit very weakly, sex of owner. In further detail:

The dollar amount of financial capital invested by the owner is clearly more important than any other owner trait when it comes to delineating active from discontinued black-owned businesses.

The second most influential factor is the owner's age; those in the 45 to 54 age bracket are much more likely to remain in business than younger or older owners. Age is undoubtedly related to general experience, up to a point: as old age sets in, general intensity of work effort declines and business viability suffers accordingly.

The third-ranked factor is leveraged debt; active firms are clearly more highly leveraged than discontinued ones. Reliance upon debt capital at the point of startup is *not* associated with heightened risk of failure. The strong, direct relationship between leverage and black firm longevity suggests that the following scenario is operating: black owners who can achieve a highly leveraged position are, in fact, extremely attractive from a credit-risk standpoint. As indicated earlier, college graduates had access to much larger bank loans than less highly educated black business owners.

Fourth factor: owners working longer hours are more likely to belong to the active business group. This is particularly applicable to owners who pursue self-employment full-time: their peers working only part-time are less likely to see their firms survive.

Fifth factor: owners with more than four years of college are more likely to see their businesses survive, but the owner education variables in fact rank lower than expected. This is partly because education has a ripple effect on other variables—total capitalization and leverage for example, since banks consider education in measuring credit worthiness. Hence education's link to business viability is both direct and indirect. The softened effect of education also stems from factors (explored in chapter five) related to the general exodus of well-educated self-employed blacks from inner-city communities.

Finally, businesses run by males are somewhat more likely to endure than firms owned by black females, though this relationship is weak.

Two firm-specific variables—firm age and buyout status—were found to be associated with business viability. Among the youngest black firms, those formed in 1982—which made up 24.0 percent of the total sample—over 38 percent had discontinued by 1986. The longer the period since the owner entered his/her business, the more likely it was that the business remained active in 1986.

The "ongoing business" variable produced an unexpected finding: firms acquired as buyouts were less likely to survive than businesses started from scratch. This may be due in part to the fact that buyouts are most often small-scale retail firms located in minority neighborhoods. These types of retailing operations have the highest rate of discontinuance observed among the various lines of black enterprise: 40 percent of those in the CBO young black firm sample had folded by late 1986. The entire sample of young black firms had a discontinuance rate of 29.0 percent; net of retailing, that rate drops to 27.7 percent.

Access to Credit and the Likelihood of Small-Business Survival

Borrowers in the black sample of young firms reported a mean financial investment of $32,813 (total), while their nonborrower cohorts began business, on average, with a much more modest $7,660 (table B.4). In light of the findings linking black firm sales levels and survival prospects to size of financial capital invested in the firm, it is tempting to conclude that more debt causes healthier, larger-scale business.

This suggests that increases in loan availability would produce increases in black business viability, independent of all other firm characteristics. This conclusion can be accepted only with important qualifications. Excessive lender caution, including redlining practices, partially shields black businesses from suffering the higher default rates often associated with the liberal lending practices many white firms encounter. And since only the very strongest black business borrowers get large loans, their consequent success could be attributed at least as much to their pre-debt soundness as to the loan itself. In sum, black business viability rises as indebtedness rises, a pattern that does not mirror the usual situation for nonminorities.

Before proceeding, it is useful to summarize what is known about those who do make large financial investments when starting their enterprises. First, for both black and white CBO business samples, debt and equity at the point of startup are complements. Second, in these samples, the single most important determinant of debt level—for white as well as black firms—is the absolute size of the entrepreneur's equity. Third, apart from equity, high educational attainment is associated with the largest loans. And fourth, as a complementary study has shown, owners receiving the largest loans are those who earned the highest personal incomes prior to entering business.[21]

The business owner who has the greatest access to debt therefore typically: (1) is highly educated, (2) has a high personal income, and (3) invests a substantial amount of equity capital into the firm. All of this suggests the following two-stage line of causation:

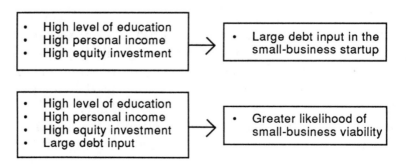

Would greater loan availability assist the weaker small businesses? The basic hypothesis that higher levels of debt increase firm viability is qualified by a countervailing trend: a high degree of debt may reduce business survival chances by raising the probability of default.[22] It is important to recall that during the late 1960s and early 1970s, the Small Business Administration (SBA) Economic Opportunity Loan (EOL) program approved many thousands of loans to high-risk minority borrowers who could not obtain loans from other sources. In our 1977 analysis of SBA loan data, Donald Hester and I[23] showed that larger loans, other things equal, were directly associated with greater chances of failure. A later study[24] found that weak, highly leveraged SBA loan recipients were more likely to fail, relative to less highly leveraged borrowers.

While those findings concerning the SBA program may seem inconsistent with the findings of this study, it is important to note that lending criteria used by the SBA were quite different from those employed by commercial banks. The point is that the findings of this chapter *do not* disprove the earlier conclusions about the folly of liberal lending to high-risk minority business borrowers.

It may indeed be true that black businesses are being handicapped by restricted access to credit, but in light of SBA's unsuccessful EOL loan program for minorities, this must be proven decisively. The matter is pursued in chapter five, which indeed does find that certain black firms are being unfairly handicapped by limited credit access.

This study has found no evidence indicating that highly leveraged firms are less likely to remain in business than other borrowers; rather, the discriminant analysis suggests that the opposite is true (see table B.6). Nonetheless, high degrees of leverage may indeed be imprudent for many business borrowers.

If capital markets refuse, however, to supply debt to such firms, then the relationship between leverage and business viability—normally an inverse relationship when firm indebtedness is high—fails to materialize. In fact, excessive lender caution does appear to be severely limiting black entrepreneurs' access to credit. In this environment, only the strongest borrowers get the largest loans, and we observe that high indebtedness is now associated with business survival rather than with default. Strength, simply stated, improves credit worthiness, and business startups tend to borrow as much as the banks will permit.

Lender caution—particularly commercial bank caution—is most pronounced in inner-city minority communities (see chapter five). In that milieu, the limited availability of credit amounts to redlining, and it severely undermines small-business prospects for the survival of white as well as black entrepreneurs.

4 THE URBAN GHETTO MILIEU

I t was in the mid-1960s—a time of protests and riots in the ghettoes of Los Angeles, Detroit, Chicago, and other large cities—that business and government leaders began discussing the need for black business development in earnest. Promoting "black capitalism" (and other minority entrepreneurship) had gained wide appeal across the political spectrum: over the ensuing 15 years, Democrats and Republicans alike would expand programs for aiding minority-owned firms through procurement and through financial and managerial assistance.[1]

Loans formed the major component of this minority business promotion until 1977, reaching their peak in numbers and dollar amounts in 1972 and 1973. Since the late 1970s, as these loan approvals declined in number, preferential procurement contracts and minority business set-aside programs have rapidly grown. Set-asides at the federal level have expanded largely because of the efforts of Congress. Minority-owned business gained an estimated $7 billion in contracts for the construction and repair of highways and other infrastructure from Congressman Parren Mitchell's amendment to the 1982 Surface Transportation Assistance Act, which required that at least 10 percent of the $70 billion spent under the act be awarded to minority firms. Similar set-asides proliferated through the 1980s at all levels of government—federal, state, and local.[2]

Reflecting the milieu in which minority business assistance was popularized, these programs have always cited the alleviation of ghetto poverty and disorder as an important rationale. The goal of increasing employment opportunities for minorities, particularly in high-unemployment ghetto areas, has consistently enjoyed wide political appeal. When introducing a set-aside provision to Congress in 1977, Sen. Edward Brooke, a black Republican from Massachusetts, stressed the need to alleviate chronic unemployment in minority communities; minority-owned firms, he claimed, drew their work forces primarily from such areas.[3] A related goal of minority business assistance has been to expand the population of minority entrepreneurs in order to provide minority youths with role models.[4] By creating jobs, encouraging success stories, and nurturing role models, black business development was, ideally, going to generate the ghetto's overall economic development.

The size and scope of the black business community has broadened considerably in the last three decades, in part due to the influx of entrepreneurs into lines of business where minority representation has historically been minimal. Yet as a group black businesses still lag far behind nonminority businesses; on average, black firms are smaller, less profitable, and more prone to failure. And this laggard performance typifies black enterprises not only in such traditional fields as personal services but in emerging growth areas as well.

In urban ghettoes the growth of black-owned businesses has been particularly slow, in some cases nonexistent. Firms located in these minority communities—whether owned by minorities or by others—have collectively failed to overcome the constraints that the ghetto milieu imposes. As a rule, the traits of these firms are the opposite of those which characterize successful businesses, discussed in the preceding chapter.

Facing limited access to financial capital, firms that most commonly survive in the ghetto are smaller in sales and employment than firms located elsewhere, and they are more likely to be headed by high school dropouts than by college graduates. The most promising entrepreneurial talent rarely remains within the ghetto's borders.

While limited access to capital and markets handicaps businesses located in the ghetto irrespective of their owners' racial background, the black business community suffers disproportionately. Business development is difficult to sustain in an environment that offers weak consumer markets and from which financial capital and highly educated people are in continual flight. This chapter discusses how the ghetto interacts with the rest of the economy in ways that hinder the ghetto's own economic growth.

Minority Firms and the Markets They Serve

Chapter three demonstrated that smaller startup investments (in both equity and debt) distinguish black owners from white owners, clearly causing black firms to be smaller and less viable. But beyond financial input, a second trait that clearly delineates black from white firms is access to markets. Black businesses typically sell to other minorities, and this is particularly true among black firms located in the ghettos of the nation's largest cities. Between 1972 and 1977, according to a study by John Handy and David Swinton, the strength of local black purchasing wielded a powerful influence on growth in black business receipts.[5] Because ghetto residents often have low and variable personal incomes, low rates of labor force participation, and high rates of unemployment, the ghetto's internal market is weak, and this weakness is reflected in the state of its business community.

When firms are divided into those whose clientele is predominantly minority and those whose clientele is mixed or nonminority, the levels of sales and employment differ systematically. This pattern is demonstrated in table 4.1, which also shows that white-owned firms serving the minority market actually have a lower survival rate than black firms in the same market. White firms do significantly better serving nonminority markets.

Traditional lines of black enterprise—typified by personal services—are largely small-scale, ghetto-based firms that serve minority customers. Fewer than 15 percent of black-owned personal service firms compete for nonminority customers. Altogether, the three lines of black enterprise that rely *most* heavily on minority clientele are personal services, retailing, and FIRE (finance, insurance, and real estate). Emerging lines of black enterprise, by contrast, tend to compete actively in the nonminority marketplace; this is especially true in three industry groups: construction, manufacturing, and business services. Among black firms doing business in large metropolitan areas, personal

Table 4.1
Comparison of CBO Firms in 28 Metropolitan Areas[a] by Minority Make-up of Markets Served: Mean Firm Size and Survival Rates

	Black-Owned Firms	White Male-Owned Firms
Serving Predominantly Minority Markets [b]		
1982 sales	$49,362	$96,501
Number of paid employees	0.6	1.0
Percent still active, 1986	73 5%	69.8%
Serving Mixed & Nonminority Markets [b]		
1982 sales	$70,211	$174,593
Number of paid employees	1.0	2.1
Percent still active, 1986	74.7%	79.0%

Source: CBO survey data (unpublished); see Appendix A for description of sample.

[a] See chapter five for a full listing of the 28 applicable metropolitan areas and the criteria used in selecting them.

[b] Firms are classified as predominantly minority-market oriented if 75 percent or more of their customers are minorities. Use of 75 percent as a cutoff point was dictated by the nature of the Census Bureau questionnaire.

services rely on the minority market the most while construction firms do so the least.

That black-owned firms in the FIRE industry are minority-oriented is an interesting exception to the traditional/emerging pattern. Finance, insurance, and real estate are emerging lines of business that have attracted highly educated black entrepreneurs. Yet it is common for black college graduates to enter skill-intensive service industries—FIRE in particular, professional services to a lesser extent—that cater to a largely minority clientele. For professionals as well as high school dropouts, then, black self-employment in the minority market is associated with very small firms and minimal growth potential. A comparison of mean 1982 sales for all blacks and whites in the CBO samples who run businesses in the FIRE industry is revealing:

F.I.R.E. industry sales (mean)

Black firms	$36,759
White male firms	$156,533

The only major sector of the service industry that has lower sales than FIRE is personal services; black-owned firms in that sector produced mean 1982 sales of $26,634.

The Inner City, the Ghetto, and Black Business Viability

To create viable small businesses, it is worth noting again, requires talented and capable entrepreneurs who have access to investment capital as well as markets for their products. The weakness of all three of these elements has traditionally handicapped many of the small firms that have operated in inner-city minority communities. In these locations neither the black-owned businesses nor the nonminority enterprises are flourishing.

The remainder of this chapter discusses how the ghetto interacts with the rest of the economy in a way that depresses the performance of inner-city businesses. The barriers that especially hinder black business in the ghetto milieu are identified and analyzed. After reviewing this context, it becomes possible (in chapter five) to link these firms' performance to the circumstances of the ghetto economy. All of this necessitates defining what a ghetto is.

Ghetto defining mechanisms. The urban ghetto is a depressed enclave within a prosperous economy. As people and income move into and out of the ghetto, the area's economy ensures that resources are rarely invested there, so that the ghetto's poverty remains as a fixed characteristic of the national economy. The pattern is one of self-reinforcing influences: poverty reinforces the conditions that lead to poverty, and resources that might lead to economic development are drained out.[6] For the larger economy, the ghetto provides a pool of laborers for society's low-wage menial occupations. Common traits that push people into this cheap labor pool include race, poor education, low skills, and/or inability to speak English. These traits, in turn, serve as barriers that block mobility outward.

The migration of former sharecroppers into Northern cities, sparked by the mechanization of cotton picking, illustrates how ghetto mechanisms work. By 1955, mechanization had caused black sharecroppers in the Mississippi Delta—poor, uneducated, possessing only agricultural skills—to become redundant in the South. The sharecropper could not easily remain in an agricultural region where employment alternatives were scarce. The whirlwinds of economic change left this displaced worker little choice but to migrate. Partly by choice, largely because there was no other place to go, he ended up in an urban ghetto. There he would find himself boxed in by barriers to upward mobility.

Low income means low levels of living: poor food, bad housing, deficient sanitation. These conditions tend to reinforce low labor productivity (particularly when they injure a worker's health), in turn perpetuating low income. Moreover, the constant drain on the ghetto's resources—manpower, capital, income—reinforces the poverty of the community as a whole. Public services that might help overcome the deficiencies in private incomes are substandard. To return to the example, not only the ex-sharecropper but his children are caught up in a system of cumulative causation—poor schools leading to low productivity, low productivity to low incomes, low incomes to poor nutrition, poor nutrition to illness, and so forth—which tends to pass on the barriers of ghettoization from one generation to the next. Life in the ghetto economy is something of a vicious circle.

Of course, the ghetto is not completely cut off from the rest of society; many residents eventually manage to move up economically and escape it. Just as the inadequate provision of public services—such as education—tends to preserve ghettoization, their adequate provision can enhance labor productivity. The intergenerational transmission of poverty is not inevitable: the sharecropper's children could, under the right circumstances, attend college. Such educational credentials would enable them to penetrate the economy's high-wage sector; they could then move out of the ghetto, having surmounted the barriers that held their parents there.

Unfortunately, for the majority of ghetto residents these barriers do prove insurmountable. Often its physical isolation limits access to employment, particularly for young adults.[7] Moreover, the mobility to move outward does not entirely depend on merit or even income; race is an important criterion. Ghetto residents are often stereotyped as personally embodying their community's worst traits—low labor force productivity, poor education, poverty, and so forth—and these stereotypes become the grounds for discriminatory treatment by potential employers.

Employers appear to devalue diplomas granted by predominantly black high schools,[8] and they sometimes associate young blacks with criminal behavior.[9] A job may be withheld from a black youth simply because she or he is assumed to be poorly educated, inexperienced, and unreliable without specific evidence to the contrary. This sort of prejudgment, or statistical discrimination, is often self-fulfilling: it denies black job seekers the work experience and the references they would need to become employable. Black youths caught in this cycle of rejection "may turn to activities and lifestyles that justify the stereotype and raise the adverse odds that similar blacks encounter in the future."[10]

The drain on income. The ghetto's chief resource is labor, and its largest flow of income derives from employment. In most ghettos, a substantial minority of the labor force hold middle-income jobs, and a few residents actually hold high-wage jobs although they are also the people most likely to move out.

Income flows out of the ghetto as residents buy goods produced elsewhere in stores that are typically owned by outsiders. Internal flows of income that might support greater economic activity and higher incomes within the ghetto are largely absent. Instead, the transference of income supports economic activity outside the ghetto. A study of the Hough neighborhood in Cleveland, which drew from household spending diaries, documented such an outflow of income through ordinary household spending. This study, published in 1971, found that for each dollar of family expenditures, only 13 cents was spent on goods and services sold by businesses located in Hough.[11] Likewise, a study of local businesses in Brooklyn's Bedford-Stuyvesant community found that in 1969 resident business owners there earned a total of $400,000 in profits from their enterprises while nonresident owners earned $14.1 million.[12] Income flows such as these exacerbate inner-city underdevelopment.[13] Too often, money passes through urban ghettos "without lingering long enough to turn over several times and thereby generate incomes for other of the community's residents," as Robert Browne describes it.[14]

In any community, the goods purchased are largely imported from elsewhere, and in this respect ghettos are like any other urban area. In most communities, however, a major portion of the retail and wholesale establishments are owned locally so that the owners' incomes are largely spent locally. The resultant chain of spending and respending has a multiplier effect, adding strength and variety to the local economy.[15] If the dollars a ghetto resident brought into his community did not leave immediately but were spent inside it several times, the additional economic activity those dollars fueled would tend to benefit other ghetto residents. If more local businesses were owned by neighborhood residents, who in turn would spend their substantial incomes within the community, even more money would circulate within the ghetto economy. This line of reasoning is part of the logic behind promoting local ownership of ghetto businesses.

The drain on housing. In most communities, purchasing power is also rechanneled back into the local economy through the ownership of rental housing by local residents. In the ghetto, however, rental housing is owned overwhelmingly by outsiders; since most of the landlords are not ghetto consumers, monthly rent checks do not come back into the ghetto to support other enterprises or employees.

The payment of rent checks probably constitutes the greatest flow of capital out of the ghetto. Moreover, landlords' minimal maintenance of this housing enables them to recoup their investment even as the buildings themselves deteriorate. This kind of housing disinvestment withdrew $25.8 million from Bedford-Stuyvesant in 1969, according to Richard Schaffer (1973).

Treating property this way ultimately makes it worthless because of wear and tear, but while it is being used up the absent owner can realize a nice cash flow while he takes out his capital. Unfortunately, "neighborhood effects" cause housing disinvestment to be a self-reinforcing process that accelerates once it begins.[16] When a few property owners fail to maintain their structures, owners of surrounding property do likewise as a matter of self-protection, since one deteriorated building draws down the value of others nearby.

Even when rental housing is owned by ghetto residents it usually undergoes the same decline, since it is subject to the same economic forces. Although local ownership tends to retain purchasing power within the community, slowing the drain on income, resident landlords may none-theless fail to maintain their property in neighborhoods where value is dropping as other buildings deteriorate.

The drain on investment funds. The development of an area's financial industry typically stimulates broader economic growth, because it mobilizes savings that would otherwise be held as idle cash balances. Households and businesses depend on the availability of such funds to finance major outlays, such as home improvements and business expansions, that they cannot pay for out of their current cash incomes.

Financial institutions that serve the ghetto, however, have traditionally done a minimal job of servicing the loan demands of ghetto households and businesses. A substan-tial portion of the area's savings goes into banks and savings and loan associations (S&Ls), whose investment policy is to use those funds for mortgages, business loans, and other investments in communities elsewhere. While ghetto residents who save undoubtedly enjoy the safety and convenience these institutions provide, local borrow-ers may not have access to the pool of savings assembled.[17] (In this regard, the continuing bank practices of redlining and racial discrimination against business borrowers con-tribute much harm; see chapter 5). In the end, little comes back to support the ghetto economy or promote its development.[18]

Increasing the ownership of banks and S&Ls by ghetto residents could, potentially, reverse this savings drain by pooling and investing the savings of area residents to finance economic development. This constitutes an important rationale for supporting the creation and expansion of minority-owned inner-city financial institutions.

Certain economic facts of ghetto life, however, constrain the behavior of *any* financial institutions that are actively collecting deposits from and lending to a ghetto clientele. Since the incomes of these bank customers are, on average, lower and less stable than those of customers elsewhere, the size of their deposit accounts is well below the national average for similar institutions. Smaller account size necessarily means more paperwork and teller labor for each deposited dollar, raising the bank's expenses relative to deposits.[19]

Banks and S&Ls that are actively lending to ghetto borrowers therefore lend to a clientele characterized by higher risk than that faced by non-ghetto lending institutions, and their performance reflects the disparities in economic well-being that distinguish inner-city minorities from the rest of society.[20] This helps to explain why black-owned banks and S&Ls have, in fact, experienced relatively high operating expenses and loan losses—as well as lower and less stable annual profits—compared to their nonminority counterparts. While this higher risk has not undermined the viability of most black-owned financial institutions, it has limited their size and scope, leaving them ill-equipped to reduce the drain on the ghetto community's savings.

The drain on labor. While the siphoning off of the ghetto's income, savings, and housing capital has long been a problem, the most serious contributor to poverty has been the drain on labor, which has grown in intensity in recent years. The ghetto's chief resource is its labor, yet the best workers have increasingly been departing by way of the educational system and the high-wage economy.

Drawn by opportunities outside the poor urban areas, many of the most intelligent, capable, and imaginative young people have moved into the economic mainstream, where rewards are greater and opportunities wider. Yet as these minorities contribute to the advancement of the dominant society,[21] the ghetto they leave behind stagnates, and most minority youth find themselves with even fewer routes of escape. The isolation of the ghetto and the drains on its talent and capital only grow worse. More and more, blacks find themselves divided into haves and have-nots— a division that corresponds to one already present in the larger society. Politically, this tends to undermine the united action of black groups; those who a generation ago would have been the leadership class of the ghetto are today increasingly divorced from its concerns.

Programs that expand access to employment and educational opportunities are certainly important and beneficial, but they can only be part of a larger solution focused on the processes by which ghettos are created and sustained. Too often, these programs are rooted in the belief that individual effort, together with public support for education and training, will solve the problem as a whole. Given that assumption, when residents unaffected by the programs remain caught in the ghetto, they are frequently told that the fault is theirs, that if they had the initiative they too could have become affluent. This mindset provides a rationale for not fully attacking the roots of the problem: the barriers and the resource drains that work to block mobility.

Black Businesses' Impact on the Draining of Ghetto Resources

One option for well-educated blacks that normally does *not* entail leaving the ghetto is business ownership. Whereas the hiring of educated minorities into the mainstream economy draws talent away, the expansion of minority ownership retains local entrepreneurial talent within the ghetto area and is therefore a prerequisite for reversing the drain on its resources and generating cumulative growth. As mentioned earlier, local ownership of businesses strengthens internal flows of income, contributing to and benefiting from multiplier effects in the region.

To envision the impact that an increase in locally owned businesses would have on the ghetto's economy, it is useful to divide the businesses into two groups: those serving predominantly a ghetto clientele (including most retail and service industries), and those serving larger markets, either the metropolitan area or, in a few instances, a national market. This second group includes many firms in the fields of manufacture, wholesale, transportation, and construction.

The success of both types of firms promotes ghetto development, though firms oriented toward local customers can do this in only a limited way. Through the jobs and income they generate, local-market firms may help to slow the resource drain, but only firms serving broader markets have the power to reverse it. The prospects of the former are limited by income levels within the ghetto; the prospects of the latter by their global competitiveness. Firms serving regional or national markets can catalyze the net inflow of resources that is so vitally needed.

Before moving on, it is worth recapitulating the characteristics of the economic environment in which minority entrepreneurs must operate. The ghetto's poverty is partially maintained by net outflows of three kinds: of capital, in forms such as savings, housing stock, and infrastructure; of income, exacerbated by weak internal income flows and a low resultant regional multiplier; and of talent, including the many intelligent, capable, and imaginative young people who leave by way of the educational system to enter the high-wage economy. As long as it remains stripped of its capital and talent, the ghetto economy has no prospect of generating jobs and incomes for its residents.

All of the outflows described in this chapter can be alleviated by the strategy of creating and expanding black-owned businesses and financial institutions, although due to lack of capital, weak markets, and related factors this approach is fraught with risks. If we are to turn toward the minority entrepreneur as part of the answer to the ghetto's economic problems, we must also examine the barriers to financing faced by black business owners and others starting up enterprises within the ghetto's boundaries. Chapter five addresses these problems.

5 FIRM LOCATION AND BANK REDLINING

The chronic economic distress of the ghetto, where many black firms are forced to survive, goes far toward explaining why, in spite of the last 25 years' progress, so much of the black business community continues to stagnate. As the last chapter illustrated, outflows of financial capital and entrepreneurial talent, in combination with weak internal markets, continue to thwart enterprise development in the inner city. Not surprisingly, the success of educated black entrepreneurs in emerging lines of business, discussed earlier in the book, has been most pronounced in locations removed from minority communities.

Even in minority communities outside the core ghetto, small-business owners who would serve minority consumers are beset by barriers that firms elsewhere do not have to contend with, such as redlining by commercial lenders. The analysis that follows compares the relative performance of black-owned businesses both inside and outside of black residential areas, providing a broader picture of their working environment.

The healthier, emerging lines of black enterprise are avoiding or moving out of inner-city minority communities, locating instead in central business districts or outlying suburbs. One of the identifiable causes of this trend is the fact that commercial banks are extensively redlining small firms that do business in minority communities. The net result is that inner-city black communities are increasingly being left out of the business development process.

Since inner-city communities are unpromising business sites, it would only seem logical to expect that minority communities outside the ghetto would offer entrepreneurs far better chances of success. In their economic and social characteristics, residents of these more affluent minority areas are often indistinguishable from the surrounding white suburban population. A much stronger base of purchasing power is potentially available there for black-owned retailers and consumer-service firms to draw on.

In fact, minority businesses in minority suburbs do not do as well as their neighborhood customer profile would lead one to expect. The advantages inherent in serving stronger internal markets are offset by restricted access to financial capital. Black firms located in all minority communities—ghetto and nonghetto alike—tend to be very small in part because their access to credit is re-stricted: they are less likely than owners in nonminority locations to borrow at all, and when they do borrow they receive substantially smaller loans. A significant part of this problem can be traced to lender discrimination against minority borrowers, discussed next, and to redlining against minority neighborhoods, discussed subsequently.

Discrimination Against Minority Borrowers: The Ando Study

Redlining by commercial banks applies to minority communities in general—not just to the core regions of the poverty ghetto that are typified by intense poverty and racial segregation. Moreover, in addition to this geo-graphic discrimination, banks are discriminating against owners: black business owners of established firms have had substantially less success than nonminorities in ob-taining commercial bank credit. This is the conclusion reached by Faith Ando's pathbreaking 1988 study, which offers the most concrete evidence of discrimination against existing black businesses by commercial lenders that is currently available.[1]

Given its importance to the subject, Ando's study is worth briefly reviewing. Until recently, no systematic data existed concerning how banks have treated the loan requests of established small businesses. Ando's study, which was sponsored by the U.S. Small Business Administration, remedies this. Ando compares bank loan availability for large national samples of small businesses owned by black, Hispanic, Asian, and nonminority entrepreneurs, looking at their success in applying for commercial bank loans over a three-year period in the early 1980s. By design, only established businesses participated in the study. Firms from all 50 states are represented. The percentages of all short-term bank loan applications that were accepted are these:

Acceptance rates for short-term loans requested by . . .

Blacks	61.7 %	
Hispanics	86.6 %	
Nonminorities	89.9 %	100%
Asians	96.2 %	

The above figures do not necessarily reflect discrimination against blacks, if, in fact, black loan applicants are higher credit risks overall than the other business groups. To test for discrimination, Ando examined the relevance of numerous factors that influence loan approval. Ando found that even when borrowers' credit risk is statistically controlled for, black businesses are much more likely to be denied commercial loans than are nonminorities, Asians, or Hispanics.

More specifically, Ando found that four conditions are the most important in ensuring loan approval: (1) the owner's having lengthy business experience; (2) the firm's size being sufficiently large; (3) an excellent credit rating; and (4) the owner's requesting shorter loan maturities rather than long ones.

Six factors Ando found to be causes of loan rejection are (1) a record of previous bankruptcy; (2) a poor credit rating or no rating at all; (3) being in the "wrong" industry, such as manufacturing (the period under consideration coincided with widespread recession in manufacturing industries); (4) the owner's being divorced; (5) the owner's needing cosigners for the loans; and (6) the owner's belonging to the "wrong" racial or ethnic group—black borrowers were less likely to achieve loan approval.

Redlining Against Minority Neighborhoods

Beyond the basic question of access to startup loans is the question of what influences banks in determining how much to lend. When most people borrow from commercial banks to establish small businesses, the amounts they are loaned depend first and foremost on the size of the equity investment they put up. A larger equity investment means more access to debt; the surest way to get a $100,000 startup loan is to invest $50,000 or so of one's own money as owner's equity. For black entrepreneurs, however, it is not their equity investment that typically has the most influence on their loan amount—it is where their firms are situated. That is the conclusion reached by the analysis conducted for this study. If the proposed business is located in a minority community, loan size is cut drastically.

This chapter documents the practice of redlining against the neighborhoods where black businesses are located. For this analysis, black businesses in 28 large metropolitan areas are further subdivided into two groups: those operating in minority neighborhoods and those located in mixed or nonminority sections. In addition to documenting redlining, the analysis of firm location turns up three other important findings. First, when their firms are located in minority neighborhoods, even highly educated black owners are much more likely than they otherwise would be to abandon self-employment. Second, while black college graduates prefer to locate their firms in nonminority locales, owners who are high school drop-outs are the owners likely to survive when they operate in the ghetto milieu.

The third finding, which concerns patterns of employment, deserves special comment. Black-owned firms, it turns out, employ minority workers to a much greater extent than white-owned firms doing business in the same areas. Black employers tend to utilize a work force consisting largely of minority workers, and this is true whether they are located in inner-city ghettos, central business districts, or outlying suburban areas. White-owned businesses behave quite differently. Among all small-business employers located in nonminority areas of the applicable 28 cities, 62.7 percent of the white firms (versus 3.1 percent of the black firms) had no minority employees at all. More surprisingly, even when located within minority communities, most white-owned firms employ predominantly nonminority workforces, and many employ no minority workers whatsoever. In sum, the evidence clearly suggests that the race of owners is a major determinant of minority workers' access to jobs in the small-business sector.

Metropolitan areas chosen for this study. The 28 SMSAs analyzed in this study all have the following traits: (1) a substantial black population, (2) identifiable ghetto areas, and (3) numerous black-owned businesses. A metropolitan area was identified as having a ghetto if it contained five or more census tracts with 1980 poverty rates of 40 percent or more.[2] The applicable metropolitan areas in this study therefore are not merely the nation's largest, although most of those having one million or more residents in 1980 did qualify for the list of 28. In fact, the above three criteria also led to the inclusion of several Southern areas with fewer than one million residents (such as Richmond, Jackson, and Nashville) as well as one small Northern area (Gary-Hammond-East Chicago, in Indiana).

The list of 28 is dominated by 14 large metropolitan areas in the sense that most of the black businesses sampled were, in fact, located in these areas. These 14 are:

Atlanta	Los Angeles
Baltimore	New Orleans
Chicago	New York
Cleveland	Philadelphia
Dallas-Fort Worth	St. Louis
Detroit	San Francisco-Oakland
Houston	Washington, D.C.

The other 14 areas are:

Birmingham	Memphis
Columbus	Milwaukee
Gary	Nashville
Indianapolis	Newark
Jackson	Omaha
Jacksonville	Richmond
Kansas City	Shreveport

It is worth noting that 10 central city governments in these 28 metropolitan areas were headed by black mayors in 1982: Los Angeles, Detroit, Washington, D.C., New Orleans, Atlanta, Oakland, Richmond, Birmingham, Newark, and Gary. A major objective of this chapter is to provide a context for the later discussion of the impact black political power has on black business development. Chapter six examines the possibility that the forces that constrain black business progress may somehow be counterbalanced by that manifestation of black political power, the black mayor; it also examines whether the derivative effects of black business development are more beneficial to residents of cities presided over by black mayors. Those questions cannot adequately be addressed, however, until the urban context—and its impact on black business viability—is explored in more depth.

Traits of the small businesses studied. The same sorts of discrepancies between black- and white-owned small businesses that were documented in chapter three are again evident in the 28 metropolitan areas reviewed here. The white-owned firms are typically much larger in sales than their black cohorts, and they were started with much greater financial investments. (See appendix C; appendix table C.1 presents summary statistics for the entire sample of black- and white-owned firms under consideration; tables C.2 through C.5, which will be referred to in the following pages, illustrate other statistical analyses relevant to this chapter.)

As expected, black firms with paid employees, which make up 23 percent of the black businesses studied, fare much better than black nonemployer firms. Mean sales in 1982 were over $150,000 for black employers, compared to just $27,445 for the nonemployers; and the survival rate (as of 1986) was 82.4 percent for employers versus 71.4 percent for nonemployers. Yet the starkest contrasts emerge when comparing black firms with white firms— employers and nonemployers alike. Not only are white firms more likely to have paid employees, their mean sales are more than twice as high and their financial investments dwarf those reported by black enterprises:

Total sales (mean), 1982

Black firms	$153,116	▬▬▬▬▬▬▬
White male firms	$393,806	▬▬▬▬▬▬▬▬▬▬▬▬▬▬▬▬

Total financial investment (mean)

Black firms	$28,204	▬▬▬▬▬▬▬▬
White male firms	$63,937	▬▬▬▬▬▬▬▬▬▬▬▬▬▬▬▬

Obtaining debt capital is enormously important to a firm's total capitalization. This is evident in tables 5.1 and 5.2, which break down capital amounts for borrower and nonborrower groups. The CBO data for firms formed between 1976 and 1982 show that borrowers, whether black or white, consistently enter business with much more financial capital than nonborrowers (table 5.1).

White-owned firms are more likely to borrow than black-owned firms, and when they do borrow, their average loan size ($41,605) is nearly double the corresponding black figure ($22,607). Moreover, most business loan dollars come from commercial banks, particularly among black borrowers: mean debt for black entrepreneurs receiving bank loans was $33,860, versus $12,543 for those borrowing from nonbank sources.

Of course, white-owned businesses are much less likely than black firms to cater to a minority clientele, and their geographic distribution differs sharply. Black firms tend to be located in inner-city minority communities, whereas white-owned enterprises rarely are. This distinction goes far toward explaining both the laggard overall performance of black enterprise and the growth trajectory of black businesses' more successful subset. Consider the figures in table 5.2, which group the study's young black firms according to location.

The greatest disparity is in debt capital: mean debt for black firms in nonminority communities was almost three times greater than that for minority-area firms. Chapter three emphasized the vast differences in financial capitalization that distinguish black businesses from white ones. Those differences are partly rooted in the fact that debt capital is much more readily available to black-owned

Table 5.1
Financial Capital, Debt Capital, and Loan Incidence Among Young Firms, by Owner Race

	Borrowers Only		Nonborrowers Only	
	Black firms	White firms	Black firms	White firms
Total financial capital (mean)	$33,937	$64,815	$8,545	$22,692
Debt capital (mean)	$22,607	$41,605	—	—
Percent receiving bank loans	47.2%	55.6%	—	—

firms located outside urban minority communities than to otherwise equally qualified firms located inside (where the bulk of black firms exist). The practice whereby firms get smaller loans because they are located in minority neighborhoods, often called redlining, is uncovered through a statistical analysis, discussed next.

Statistical evidence of redlining. The questions addressed by this analysis are straightforward: among business borrowers who are otherwise identical in age, education, equity investment, and so forth, does the borrower whose firm is located in a minority community receive a smaller loan? If so, is the difference significant? By employing multiple linear regression models (see table C.2), the relative importance to loan size of a firm's location can be clearly separated out from other owner traits. The analysis shows that startup firms in minority communities are being redlined, and that the amounts that they are denied in the form of forgone debt capital are quite significant.

Overall, it is assumed that, in the case of small-business startups, loan amounts are decided upon as a supply-side dominated matter. Lenders such as commercial banks are expected to approve larger loans to stronger borrowers, those who possess relatively large investments of equity capital and whose owner traits suggest greater viability. While weaker borrowers may have a greater demand for

Table 5.2

Financial Capital, Debt Capital, and Owner Education Among Young Black Firms: Minority vs. Nonminority Location

	Black Firms Located in Minority Communities	Black Firms Located in Nonminority Areas
Total financial capital (mean)	$15,096	$27,865
Debt capital (mean)	$5,994	$16,859
Percent of owners with four or more years of college	27.4%	41.3%

credit, particularly to overcome their lack of equity capital, lenders' aversion to risk is expected to limit the loans they give out to less attractive borrowers. A study by Scott and Dunkelberg[3] reported that very small firms received, on average, only 50 percent of their initial loan requests. Geographic location aside, it is expected that the stronger borrower will get the larger loan; debt and equity are expected to be complements rather than substitutes.

The choice of owner traits measured in this econometric exercise was shaped by chapter three's findings on business viability. Attractive owner traits include (1) high levels of education, (2) owners' ages being in the middle—rather than on the extreme ends—of the age distribution, and (3) significant managerial experience. In addition, it is expected that the purchase of ongoing firms is viewed by bank officers as a likely shortcut to business viability (although this relationship was not confirmed in chapter three). Businesses located in minority communities are hypothesized to receive smaller loans, whether the firm in question is owned by whites or blacks, because bankers assume that urban minority neighborhoods provide an unfavorable environment for most types of business.

After controlling for owner equity investment, demographic traits, and traits regarding skill, education, and experience, the black business from a minority community receives an estimated $39,564 less in loan funds than the equivalent black business from a nonminority area. This is the essence of redlining. It is the *location* of one's firm that is the *largest single determinant* of loan size for the black business that receives a bank loan.

As long as their firms are not situated in minority communities, highly educated owners with large investments of equity capital can typically expect to receive larger bank loans. Equity capital also has a most significant effect (table C.2). Black firms on average have less equity capital than their white counterparts and for that reason alone could expect to receive less debt capital. Moreover, these same black owners are less likely to be college graduates: 33.6 percent of them had completed four or more years of college, versus 45.6 percent of their white cohorts.

Nonetheless, the analysis of the 28 metropolitan areas shows that equity capital and minority location are the most influential factors in accounting for differences in the size of loans awarded. While the white bank loan recipient is awarded $1.79 in debt capital for every dollar he (or she) puts up in equity, other things being normal, the black business borrower is awarded only $0.89. This suggests that all of the black owners borrowing from banks—not just those in minority communities—are being underfunded relative to their white counterparts. Differential commercial bank treatment of black and white business borrowers accounts for most of the difference in mean debt amounts—$49,679 for whites, $33,860 for blacks—and this is particularly applicable for firms located in minority neighborhoods.

Treatment of neighborhoods with different concentrations of minorities. The finding that loan size depends on whether a black firm has a minority-neighborhood location is, statistically, highly significant, and it is not contingent on how minority neighborhoods are defined. Even where minority populations are not in the majority, the relationship between location and loan size holds as long as minorities are a significant part of the community.

This was tested by repeating the above analysis several times, each time applying a different minority-population concentration as the criterion for labeling the zip-code areas as "minority": concentrations of 50 percent or more and of 40 to 49 percent. It turns out that banks do discriminate against firms situated in zip code areas where the minority residents make up less than 50 but more than 40 percent of the total, neighborhoods where black firms are quite frequent.

Redlining against white firms. White firms seem to be redlined in minority locations along with black firms, though the evidence is sparse. Most black firms are located in areas that are 50-percent-plus minority, and in these same areas white male firms are nearly nonexistent. Only five of the white business borrowers analyzed in table C.2 are located in such neighborhoods; their small number makes statistical proof of redlining very difficult. One way to overcome this limitation, however, is by looking to see if white firms are restricted to increasingly smaller loan amounts as their neighborhoods show higher percentages of minority residents.

When this is done—utilizing minority cutoff points of 20 percent, 40 percent, and 50 percent to define "minority area" in the regression equation—the resulting statistics show the following levels of loan reduction for white firms (measured as the amount below the mean loan size for white business-loan recipients of $49,679):

Definition of Locale	Loss in Loan Amount for White Firms
20% to 39% minority population	- $ 4,180
40% to 49% minority population	- $ 9,594
50% or more minority population	- $16,782

As minority population rises, white-owned firms in the area receive smaller and smaller loans. Thus, white borrowers appear to be redlined by banks—although to a lesser degree than black-owned firms. Unfortunately, small sample size makes it difficult to confirm the statistical significance of this relationship.

To check on those findings, the same regression equation can be reestimated for a pooled sample of all 519 black and white bank loan recipients (with binary variables for minority area and race of owner). Two conclusions emerge from this exercise: (1) Business borrowers located in minority areas—whether black or white—receive an estimated $35,489 less than borrowers in nonminority communities; even when all other factors are held constant, the differences in loan size attributable to firm location are statistically significant;

(2) After controlling for minority location and other factors, the owner's race has an effect on loans; black owners are found to receive smaller loans, but this relationship was not statistically significant.

In sum, bank redlining against minority communities does go on, handicapping black-owned businesses disproportionately because that is where most of them are located. A remaining question may be asked: Are black owners discriminated against by lenders if they do business in nonminority areas? The evidence from this study does not show significant discrimination of that type, in part because the number of black business loan recipients in those areas is so small that no pattern can be confirmed with statistical confidence.

Nevertheless, potential borrowers may indeed be discriminated against at an earlier stage in the lending process—the point at which bankers decide whether to accept or reject loan applications. The previously discussed study by Ando (1988) documented this type of discrimination. The 28-city analysis conducted for this study offers some corroborating evidence—finding that among all firms doing business in nonminority communities, black firms are less likely than white firms to receive any bank loans (irrespective of amount); at the same time, the data at hand are not sufficient to distinguish between firms that were denied loans and those that might have needed but never applied for loans.

How Business Survival Traits Differ Inside and Outside Minority Communities

The discriminant analysis findings in this section corroborate earlier findings, suggesting that in the minority communities of the 28 regions studied, the prospects for black businesses are quite dismal. This particular group of firms clearly has the least access to financial capital relative to other black firms as well as to white male businesses. In addition, these firms are characterized by the very traits that, as chapter three illustrated, hamper development the most: they are the smallest, utilize the fewest employees, and are more likely to remain in business by catering to a predominantly minority clientele. And in complete contrast to the norm for small-firm startup among black firms in minority areas, those run by the least educated owners are the most likely to remain in business.

Very few firms can survive on minimal financial investments, minimal owner education and skill, and a clientele that excludes most higher-income customers. Personal services (including beauty parlors) are a significant exception. Compared to all other black industry groups, personal services are (1) most concentrated in minority areas, (2) least reliant on nonminority clients, and (3) smallest in the investment of financial startup capital. Although their mean 1982 sales per firm were the lowest reported by any industry group, black-owned personal service firms reported higher survival rates over the 1982 to late 1986 period than other black firms (as well as the sample of all white male businesses).

Survival is one thing; development is quite another. The black firms with the best prospects of development are those located *outside* minority communities. Among these black businesses, one observes larger scale, more viable firms run by generally well educated owners—over half of their owners have attended college. They are most likely to remain active if (1) they were started by owners with four or more years of college, (2) they made larger investments of financial capital, and (3) their clientele is racially diverse.

Methodology. In order to sort out which traits of the black firms in the 28 chosen metropolitan areas are most closely linked to the firms' viability, a discriminant analysis similar to that employed in chapter three is utilized. Chances of survival are expected to be influenced not only by owner traits but, given what the previous analyses have shown, by business location and the minority composition of clientele as well. As in chapter three, the measure of firm viability is, by definition, whether or not the businesses (which all began operating between 1976 and 1982) were still operating in late 1986.

The black sample of business startups is divided into two groups—those located in minority communities and those located elsewhere—and discriminant functions are estimated for each of these subsamples. Due to the very small number of white firms located in minority areas, the white sample was not similarly divided; instead, "minority area" was used as an explanatory variable. Appendix tables C.3 and C.4 list the resulting coefficients, which indicate the relative importance to firm survival of the owner traits.

Survival traits: overview. Certain universal traits are consistently and strongly linked to firm survival for all firms analyzed—black as well as white, minority as well as nonminority location. These include: (1) having been started up with substantial owner investments of financial capital—both debt and equity; (2) being an established firm (in business for at least three years); and (3) the owner's working full-time in the business.

The importance of other survival traits differs for blacks and whites, particularly in the case of leverage. While for white firms being highly leveraged (i.e., heavily in debt) raises the probability of business failure, for black firms at all locations, the pattern is the exact opposite (see table C.3). This analysis is consistent with that discussed in chapter three, which found that highly leveraged black firms consistently appear to be the strongest.

Being highly leveraged is not the only survival trait where the pattern among black firms reverses the usual pattern among white firms: In the topsy-turvy business environment of the minority community, the least educated owners are the ones most likely to remain in business, as well as those who rely most heavily on a minority clientele. In nonminority business environments, the exact opposite patterns prevail for both black and white firms.

The impact of leverage and education. Firms started with very little capital are often too small to compete for nonminority customers, particularly in the government and corporate procurement markets. Their only potential customer base lies in the minority community. Note in table C.3 that among black firms the mean value for leverage is lowest for firms located in minority communities (1.695 for discontinued firms) and highest for active firms located in nonminority areas (3.105). Also note that among black owners the discontinued firms as a group were much less highly leveraged than the surviving firms. Those firms viewed as more viable at startup—such as emerging firms that can serve a broad clientele in nonminority areas—are the ones that have greater access to debt and can therefore (1) borrow more heavily than their weaker counterparts and (2) create larger scale operations. It is not surprising that in the end these are the firms most likely to survive.

As discussed earlier (see chapter three), the fact that greater leverage corresponds with business survival positively for black owners but negatively for whites (table C.4) is completely consistent with the finding that financial capital is less accessible for black owners. Only the strongest black borrowers obtain business loans, whereas for white borrowers lending tends to be more lenient and the attendant risk is highest for those who borrow most heavily.

Nationwide, for business startups in general, those that remain active are most likely to be run by highly educated owners; owners who are high school dropouts are least associated with viable businesses. The exception to this rule occurs among black owners operating in the minority community, where dropouts are the group directly associated with business viability. The explanation may lie in the narrow options faced by black entrepreneurs who have dropped out of high school. Few highly educated blacks are willing to restrict themselves to a redlined, capital-starved minority community when greater opportunities are available elsewhere. Overall, the prospect of running a tiny firm catering to a minority clientele makes sense mostly to those who have few alternative opportunities in the broader economy: high school dropouts.

Buyout status and owner's age also have widely diverging impacts on the black and white business samples. Purchasing an ongoing firm appears to be a shortcut to business viability for white owners but not for black owners. This may be explained in part by owner assistance; buyouts are frequently financed by loans from former owners, a practice that is three times as common among white business buyers as it is among their black counterparts. The relative weakness of black buyouts may also be explained by the fact that in minority areas buyouts are concentrated in the high-risk retail sector. Finally, the owner's age is generally more important as an explanatory factor in business survival for black owners than for whites. Blacks in the 45-to-54 age bracket are more likely to remain in business than their younger or older cohorts.

Conclusion: The Prospects for Economic Development in the Ghetto

Within minority communities, capital access is constrained and the black business startups that survive consist disproportionately of tiny firms serving a purely minority clientele. Firms that stay in business in this milieu are run by those with the least education: high school dropouts who often hang on by running very small firms, such as beauty parlors, that typically have few or no paid employees. Many of these firms may be incapable of competing in the broader marketplace. No matter how long they remain active, such firms can do little to alleviate the ghetto's economic underdevelopment.

Unless greater financial capital is forthcoming and better educated owners can be induced to keep their firms there, the black business community that is located in the urban minority neighborhoods is going to stagnate, and the ghetto will continue to suffer from its endless cycle of economic drains. Unfortunately, the capital and talent that have evolved in the nation's black business community have increasingly gone into firms located either in central business districts or in outlying (and largely nonminority) suburban areas. The analyses show that the most sought-after business locations do not necessarily differ for owners of different races or ethnic origins: all businesses prosper most in environs where financial capital and markets are readily accessible. For the black (or white) college graduate seeking to start a viable business, the rationally preferred location is likely to continue to be outside the minority community.

Minority employment. Even businesses that locate in central business districts can generate net inflows of resources into minority communities if, in fact, they expand job opportunities for the residents of those communities. Wage income is the main source of cash that flows into these areas. In fact, black-owned firms are the only group that employs minorities predominantly, while white firms follow an entirely opposite pattern of hiring. (See table C.5.) The following figures highlight these clearcut differences in hiring patterns:

Employers in minority communities that . . .

have no minority employees
Black firms	1.9	
White firms	32.9	

have 50 percent or more minority employees
Black firms	96.2	
White firms	37.6	

100 %

Among white-owned small businesses in general, well over half of those that hire paid workers have no minority employees at all, and as the above figures show, even among white employers in minority communities, nearly one third have no minority workers on their payrolls. By contrast, nearly all black firms have minority workers, with 93.1 percent of black employers relying on minority workers for 75 percent or more of their employees.

The pattern holds regardless of where businesses are located. Even in the nonminority sections of the large metropolitan areas analyzed here, 86.7 percent of black-owned firms have work forces that are 50 percent-plus minority, and most had 75 percent-plus minority work forces. Among the white-owned small businesses in these same areas, most firms have no minority employees whatsoever. The prevalence of minority employees in black firms also holds regardless of firm type: it typifies large as well as small firms, white-collar industries like finance and insurance as well as blue-collar industries like manufacturing and construction. Among white firms, it is only in the manufacturing and construction industries that minority employment is widespread.

Politics and government contracts. Job creation, however important, is not synonymous with economic development. The most important barriers to inner-city development may be political rather than economic: markets *can* be found for larger scale ghetto enterprises, especially through minority business set-aside and procurement programs. To date, however, such programs have most benefited those minority firms that are located in nonminority sections of urban America.

Both as a lender and as a contractor, government regularly serves as a source of financial capital for various industries and interest groups, both domestically and abroad. Yet government's minority assistance efforts, such as the Small Business Administration's loan programs, have focused primarily on very small firms, the ones with little potential for contributing to their communities' economic development.[4] Of course, decisions about the use of public resources are made primarily by people who do not reside in urban minority communities themselves; in normal times, it is easiest for them to ignore ghetto problems.

The mayor of a large city, however, might not be able to ignore the concerns of its minority neighborhoods if, in fact, these communities are a major part of the mayor's political constituency. It is possible, then, that cities run by black mayors provide a politically friendlier environment for black-owned businesses. Testing this hypothesis is the purpose of the next chapter.

6 BLACK MAYORS AND THE IMPACT OF SET-ASIDES

T his chapter investigates the hypothesis that the growth of procurement business targeted to minorities should induce entrepreneurs to create larger-scale firms in emerging lines of business. The lure of market opportunity should discourage minority firms from entering business as tiny enterprises serving a minority clientele, since opportunities would become most prevalent for those serving corporate and government needs.

Evidence from case studies suggests that black mayors today place a high priority on municipal contracting with minority-owned businesses. Indeed, promoting black-owned businesses was ranked as "very important" by 86 percent of black elected officials.[1] Until now, however, there has been no hard evidence linking the policies of black mayors to the overall health of minority business. If the urban areas where black mayors preside do indeed offer greater opportunities than other urban areas, this should be reflected in the traits of self-employed blacks and the firms they are creating.

In fact, as the following analysis shows, they do offer greater opportunities. The analysis examined the performance of all emerging lines of black business—the established firms as well as the younger ones—comparing those in metropolitan areas governed by black mayors with those in areas governed by other mayors. It revealed that, relative to black firms elsewhere, those located in the black-mayor areas are much larger in sales and employment levels, are more likely to be run by college graduates, are being started up with much larger financial capital investments, and are failing at lower rates. Progress is most apparent among the younger firms.

The Nature of Minority Business Assistance

City governments have at their disposal numerous ways of promoting minority business development. The most powerful tool is the set-aside: most commonly, a piece of legislation will specify that a percentage of certain municipal procurement outlays must accrue to minority businesses. A complementary approach that is also common entails appointing procurement officials whose explicit mandate is to help minority businesses secure municipal contracts. In these matters the power of the mayor is considerable. Mayors may initiate programs to aid minority enterprise without the benefit of formal legislation; executive orders requiring that municipal agencies increase their purchases from minority firms have been a frequent example of this in recent years.

The mayor's appointment powers are one of the most powerful tools for assisting minority business development. Special districts control many of the functions of local government—parks, sanitation, mass transit, etc.—and mayors often appoint the directors or commissioners of these districts. In Los Angeles, for example, entrepreneurs belonging to the South Los Angeles Black Businessmen's Association have received appointments to special districts that control significant procurement dollars—such as the airport commission. These special districts, in turn, often set up their own minority procurement programs.

Of course, the mere presence of an expanding black business community does not, by itself, demonstrate that the mayor's office has had a positive effect. In a given city the existence of a substantial black business sector might predate a black mayor's tenure, which itself might conceivably have been influenced by the vibrancy of the black business constituency. The most direct evidence that black leverage in City Hall benefits black-owned firms is derived by studying businesses formed after the mayor has entered office. Consider the critically important appointment powers of the mayor. Although proponents of set-aside programs can only be placed in authoritative positions in agencies and on boards as fast as vacancies become available, between 1973 and 1980, "the black share of administrators rose from 13 to 35 percent in Atlanta and from 12 to 41 percent in Detroit."[2]

Growth of procurement opportunities targeted to black-owned businesses would therefore have to be a consequence of two sequential events in the applicable urban areas: (1) the election of the black mayor, and (2) the appointment of officials who could promote procurement programs for minority enterprise. The creation of contract opportunities would then lure potential entrepreneurs into self-employment. Those who responded by creating firms would likely be college graduates who would make large financial investments in their new businesses. The analysis that follows shows that the more substantive black businesses of this type that are emerging and successfully entering the market for procurement contracts are disproportionately doing so in the urban areas influenced by presiding black mayors. This suggests that black political power is indeed yielding new business opportunities.

Curbing abuses. When they were first introduced, minority preferential procurement and set-aside programs suffered from excessively vague eligibility criteria: procurement contracts targeted to minorities often accrued to "salt-and-pepper" businesses. Nominally, these firms were 50 percent owned by minorities, but their true owners and controllers frequently were nonminorities. In such firms the minority partner usually had no voice in managing the business, and the nonminority partner often terminated the "partnership" after the set-aside contract ended.

Government officials who administer preferential procurement programs assist legitimate minority businesses greatly when they weed out such minority front firms. The programs that have most effectively dealt with this problem have done so by confirming, for businesses whose ownership is racially mixed, that the minority partners have a capital stake and earnings commensurate with their claimed proportion of ownership. Non-trivial penalties, including fines and debarment from future government contracts, have been imposed on contractors and suppliers who established ineligible minority firms to circumvent the programs' intent.

Cities such as Atlanta and Los Angeles have been leaders in expanding the volume of procurement dollars targeted to minority enterprises. Oakland, California, is an example of a city that has actively curbed abuses by salt-and-pepper firms that too often have undermined the intent of (and weakened public support for) these minority assistance efforts.

Factors That Limit Firms' Access to Procurement

The majority of all black-owned businesses cannot directly benefit from targeted procurement programs. In all the relevant 28 metropolitan areas, the most common line of business startup for black entrepreneurs in the 1976–1982 period was small-scale retailing. By 1986, 40.6 percent of these retail operations had already closed down; this high rate of discontinuance typified firms in both the black-mayor areas and the other areas. This is not surprising, since by nature these firms do not compete for set-aside contracts: lacking both government and business markets, they sell directly to individual consumers. Whether or not five percent of government procurement dollars is set aside for minorities has no relevance to these businesses. Policy choices made in the mayor's office cannot much affect their survival or health.

In light of this, certain lines of black enterprise were excluded from the analysis—namely, all personal service and retail firms as well as the small number of firms in the agriculture, mining, forestry, and "not classified" fields. All the emerging fields—skill-intensive service fields as well as wholesaling and manufacturing—are included, since they are clearly the potential beneficiaries of procurement. Important lines of business that do not fit neatly into either the emerging or the traditional groupings were also included. Construction firms, for example, are frequently started with small amounts of financial capital by owners who have not attended college, yet construction was observed (in chapter three) to be the line of black enterprise that relied most heavily on the open market for clients. Construction firms are therefore included in the comparative analysis of emerging black firms. Businesses in transportation and "other services" industries similarly do not fit easily into either the traditional or the emerging groupings, but because they can potentially benefit from set-aside opportunities, they are included as well.

Even in the emerging fields, participation in preferential programs is seriously limited by other barriers. Over half of the black emerging firms in the areas studied have set up small-scale businesses in minority neighborhoods, and their clientele has been predominantly minority. As chapter five indicated, the record of these firms has not been good. Well-educated blacks are disproportionately abandoning self-employment in these neighborhoods. With their shrinking supply of entrepreneurial talent and limited access to commercial bank credit, it is not at all clear that inner-city minority businesses (even those in the right fields) can be competitive in the struggle for government contracts.

In nonminority sections of these metropolitan areas, a stronger group of black firms in emerging lines of business is relying increasingly upon a clientele that is either racially diverse or largely nonminority. Owners of these firms, as shown in chapter five, tend to be better educated and much more successful at raising financial capital, and their firms are typically larger than the others operating in minority communities.

Most set-aside and preferential procurement spending, according to a previous study, accrues to larger minority firms working in emerging lines of business.[3] Construction firms were the most common type competing for those contracts; firms in manufacturing and wholesaling were also heavily overrepresented, while firms in skill-intensive service fields were moderately overrepresented.[4] Nearly all of these minority firms had annual sales exceeding $100,000 and most used paid employees. All of this suggests that certain lines of minority enterprise, such as large-scale construction companies and wholesalers, are likely to capture most of the set-aside and preferential procurement business.

Black Mayors and Black Business Viability

If black mayors as a group are in fact successful in channeling increased procurement dollars to black businesses, then the most obvious beneficiaries would be the large-scale firms operating in emerging fields. In order to identify the larger-scale businesses, table 6.1 breaks the firms into employers and nonemployers. Of the applicable 28 metropolitan areas (identified in chapter five), the 10 areas with presiding black mayors in 1982 were Atlanta, Birmingham, Detroit, Gary, Los Angeles, Newark, New Orleans, Oakland, Richmond, and Washington, D.C.[5] Comparison among the black employers reveals that those in areas with presiding black mayors are substantially larger, on average, than those in the other 18 areas. No corresponding difference in size, however, is evident among the nonemployer business groups. This supports the hypothesis that the larger minority businesses are the ones benefiting disproportionately from preferential procurement.

Relative to firms in the other 18 areas, the black-mayor group of employer firms reported mean 1982 sales that were 51.9 percent higher, mean employee numbers that were 87 percent higher, and business failure rates that were somewhat lower. Further, the majority of the employers in the black-mayor group did not rely upon a predominantly minority clientele, whereas 54.8 percent of employers in the other group did.

All of these numbers are consistent with the hypothesis that black mayors in the 10 urban areas under consideration are promoting black business more effectively than their counterparts in the 18 other urban areas. Nonetheless, these numbers by themselves are not sufficient to prove the hypothesis. If black mayors' policies have had strong beneficial effects, this should be reflected in distinct patterns of success among newer black firms (those

Table 6.1

Traits of Emerging Black Firms and Their Owners in Areas With Black Mayors vs. Areas With Other Mayors: Employers vs. Nonemployers

	Areas With Black Presiding Mayors	Areas With Other Presiding Mayors
Employer Firms:		
Business traits (mean values)		
Total sales, 1982	$160,022	$105,361
Number of employees, 1982	4.3	2.3
Owner traits		
Percent having four or more years of college	40.3%	37.9%
Total financial capital (mean)	$22,860	$31,324
Percent of firms still operating in 1986	82.7%	81.0%
Number of firms:	139	153
Nonemployer Firms:		
Business traits (mean values)		
Total sales, 1982	$22,389	$25,756
Number of employees, 1982	0.0	0.0
Owner traits		
Percent having four or more years of college	33.2%	28.4%
Total financial capital (mean)	$17,993	$11,196
Percent of firms still operating in 1986	74.2%	72.0%
Number of firms	446	529

established between 1976 and 1982), which have formed and grown during the tenure of these political leaders. The 1976 cutoff point for identifying new firms is appropriate because it reflects a point in time when black mayors had been in office for several years, particularly in the larger cities—Atlanta, Detroit, Los Angeles, Washington, D.C.— where black-owned businesses are especially numerous.

This second analysis does show that black emerging firms are flourishing due to black mayors' more favorable business milieu. These young black emerging firms (see table 6.2) are larger both in size and in scope than their counterparts in the other 18 metropolitan areas:

Mean firm sales, by location

| Black-mayor areas | $53,793 | |
| Other-mayor areas | $35,953 | |

Number of employees per firm (mean)

| Black-mayor areas | 0.8 | |
| Other-mayor areas | 0.4 | |

Furthermore, lower rates of business failure typify the younger startups in the black mayor group: 27.1 percent of them had discontinued by late 1986, versus 33.1 percent of corresponding firms in the other group.

Particularly noteworthy is the difference in the mean financial investment made during startup: for firms in the black-mayor group this investment is 34.5 percent larger than for firms in the other group. Among older, more established black firms in emerging fields, no such differences in startup investment are apparent. The larger size of the businesses formed in the 10 black-mayor areas reflects the greater market opportunities there. Chapter three argued that larger scale, more viable firms in emerging fields were being created because better educated black entrepreneurs were investing substantial financial capital in them.

The increasing creation of such firms reflects both a softening of traditional constraints—such as narrow access to advanced education and training—and a growth in incentives. The greater incentives offered by preferential procurement policies in areas where black mayors are presiding are consistent with the observed pattern of new firm creation. The fact that these larger scale firms are more likely to remain in business, relative to their cohorts in the other 18 areas, is further evidence of a favorable climate for black enterprise that has evolved under the administration of black mayors.

The Persistence of Redlining

Nonetheless, problems persist for the black emerging firms, particularly with respect to amassing the financial

Table 6.2
Traits of Younger* Emerging Black Firms and Their Owners in Areas With Presiding Black Mayors vs. Other-Mayor Areas

	Areas With Black Presiding Mayors	Areas With Other Presiding Mayors
Business traits (mean values)		
Total sales, 1982	$53,793	$35,953
Number of employees, 1982	0.8	0.4
Percent of firms with paid employees	20.8%	20.1%
Owner traits		
Percent having four or more years of college	38.3%	33.8%
Total financial capital (mean)	$25,432	$18,915
Percent receiving bank loans	17.9%	23.0%
Percent of firms still operating in 1986	72.9%	66.9%
Number of firms	347	417

*Firms formed between 1976 and 1982.

capital needed to launch a large-scale business venture. Chapter five demonstrated that black owners starting firms in minority communities were the ones most likely to face barriers when raising funds for business investment. The evidence indicates that black mayors have absolutely no leverage when it comes to businesses being redlined by commercial banks. In fact, among all black emerging firms, those in areas with black mayors had worse luck obtaining bank loans than those in the other areas. Among young black emerging firms, 17.9 percent in black-mayor areas received bank loans, a figure that is far below the 23.0 percent of corresponding firms in the other areas (table 6.2) and that is even low relative to the corresponding number for all black firms.

Detroit showed the worst loan access of all: less than 10 percent of the emerging black businesses there received loans. (Even if the troubled years of the early 1980s are dropped from consideration, Detroit still ranks decisively last in terms of bank financing received by black business startups.) After Detroit, Atlanta ranked next to lowest

Table 6.3
Loan Access and Owner Education for Emerging Black Businesses* for 10 Largest Metro Areas

	Percent of Black Business Startups Receiving Bank Loans	Percent of Black Owners With Four or More Years of College
Dallas	22.4	20.7
Philadelphia	21.9	42.5
Houston	19.5	20.7
New York City	19.4	33.9
Oakland	19.1	33.8
Los Angeles	18.7	40.9
Chicago	18.6	28.9
Washington, D.C.	17.4	40.2
Atlanta	16.3	32.6
Detroit	9.9	32.9

*Both the younger black-owned firms (formed between 1976 and 1982) and the older, pre-1976 firms are analyzed in this table.

(table 6.3). The typical redlining pattern is evident in the black-mayor cities: 23.7 percent of the young emerging black firms located in nonminority sections received loans, versus a mere 15.0 percent of those located in the minority neighborhoods.

The disparity in loan access cannot be attributed to low equity investments by the black business owners. Particularly among the younger firms, mean values for equity

---

Equity investment by black-owned firms, by location

Firms in minority neighborhoods

Within black-mayor areas	$14,437	████████████████████
Within other-mayor areas	$ 6,784	██████████

Firms in nonminority neighborhoods

Within black-mayor areas	$17,056	██████████████████████████
Within other-mayor areas	$10,105	████████████████

---

investment were actually much higher for the firms started in the black-mayor areas:

Similarly, the paucity of bank financing in the black-mayor areas cannot be rooted in differences in owner education. In fact, college graduates are relatively more numerous among black entrepreneurs in the black-mayor cities than elsewhere. The city-by-city ranking in table 6.3—listing percentages of black business owners with four or more years of college—shows an even greater range than the ranking of bank loan access.

A regional difference is clearly apparent in the case of Texas; the proportions of college graduates in Dallas and Houston are very low relative to those in the other eight areas. By comparing the proportion of college-educated owners among all black emerging firms (table 6.3) with the proportion among young firms only, it is also possible to see in which cities educated entrepreneurs are an expanding portion of the business community. Their proportion is increasing most rapidly in Washington, D.C., Atlanta, and Detroit. When only younger firms are considered, Philadelphia drops from first to fourth place in the owner-education ranking. The areas that moved out in front of Philadelphia in this ranking were, in every case, areas where black mayors were presiding: Washington, D.C.

Table 6.4
Traits of Young* Business Owners in Black-Mayor Areas and Other Areas: Firms in Minority Locations Versus Those in Nonminority Locations

	Areas With Black Presiding Mayors	Areas With Other Presiding Mayors
Firms in Minority Locations:		
Owner Financial Capital Inputs (mean values)		
Total financial capital	$21,609	$13,536
Equity	14,437	6,784
Debt	7,173	6,752
Debt as a percentage of total financial capital	33.2%	49.9%
Owner Educational Background		
Percent with less than four years of high school	13.7%	18.6%
Percent having four or more years of college	32.2%	31.1%
Number of firms	233	280
Firms in Nonminority Locations:		
Owner Financial Capital Inputs (mean values)		
Total financial capital	$33,246	$29,909
Equity	17,056	10,105
Debt	16,190	19,804
Debt as a percentage of total financial capital	48.7%	66.2%
Owner Educational Background		
Percent with less than four years of high school	11.4%	13.9%
Percent having four or more years of college	50.9%	39.4%
Number of Firms	114	137

*Firms formed between 1976 and 1982 only.

(with 46.4 percent headed by college graduates), followed, in order, by Detroit and Los Angeles.

Growth in the incidence of black firms headed by college-educated owners was particularly pronounced in nonminority locations within the 28 areas under consideration (table 6.4). Consistent with this, firms started in nonminority areas also benefited from larger investments of owners' financial capital. As chapter five indicated, access to debt capital is limited for firms in minority areas, and this limitation operates with greater severity in the 10 black-mayor regions than it does in the other 18 regions. If one looks only at young black emerging firms receiving bank loans, mean debt figures were $18,618 for those in minority locations and $59,922 for those in nonminority locations.

These huge loan differences, combined with the greater incidence of nonborrowers in minority neighborhoods, mean that many firms are simply not competitive. Black business startups that might otherwise be competitive in the government procurement marketplace are undoubtedly handicapped by their limited access to debt capital. With little or no access to capital, entrepreneurs tend to create tiny businesses, which in turn have very high failure rates. Limited access to loans also depresses the overall formation rate among black firms, particularly in such capital-intensive fields as manufacturing. Owners seeking to establish large-scale firms that could be competitive in the preferential procurement marketplace must compensate when they cannot obtain needed loan dollars by investing larger sums of equity. If equity is not available, startup is often unfeasible—and potential firms never get beyond the planning stage.

Concluding Remarks

After the sorting-out period that typifies the early years of any small business, a certain group of firms remains that accounts for most of the black business community's sales and employment. These surviving firms are disproportionately located in areas where black mayors preside. Table 6.5 summarizes the 1982 traits of black firms with paid employees that were still in business in late 1986. The surviving firms in the black-mayor areas were stronger than those in the other 18 areas in every respect except for level of financial capital investment.

Particularly striking is the high survival rate of firms operating in a black-mayor milieu. Business discontinuance among emerging firms in nonminority locations was only 10.9 percent in the black-mayor group, a rate that is much lower than the 17.9 percent discontinuance rate observed in the other 18 metropolitan areas. It is even low relative to the discontinuance rate for all white-owned firms with paid employees. This extraordinarily low business failure rate reflects the fact that businesses in this category—large, emerging firms in cities governed by black mayors—are the ones that benefit disproportionately from set-asides and preferential procurement programs.

Table 6.5
Surviving Firms—Traits of Firms Still Operating in 1986: Areas With Black Mayors vs. Areas With Other Mayors (Employer Firms in Emerging Fields Only)

	Areas With Black Presiding Mayors	Areas With Other Presiding Mayors
Business Traits (mean values)		
Total sales, 1982	$175,334	$117,564
Number of employees, 1982	4.5	2.4
Owner Traits		
Percent having four or more years of college	44.3%	38.7%
Total financial capital (mean)	$25,870	$34,214
Firms Discontinuing Between 1982 and 1986		
Percent of firms in minority locations only	20.4%	21.3%
Percent of firms in nonminority locations only	10.9%	17.9%
Number of firms	115	124

7 PUBLIC POLICY THAT WOULD MAKE A DIFFERENCE

G iven the multitude of barriers to black business development, what public policy options offer the best hope? The policy discussion that follows draws upon this book's finding that a vibrant, growing black business community is best promoted by well-educated entrepreneurs whose businesses have the broadest possible access both to markets and to financial capital.

Minority Business Set-Asides in the Wake of *Richmond* v. *Croson*

Over the last two decades, the most noteworthy change in market access for black firms has been brought about by the growth of set-asides and procurement efforts targeted specifically at minorities. As discussed earlier, large corporations in consumer products industries have targeted procurement dollars to minority firms, and government set-asides for minorities now constitute a multibillion-dollar market. Government agencies have often subsidized private groups, such as the National Minority Supplier Development Council, which in turn have encouraged minority set-aside programs throughout the corporate sector. At the local level, the rise of black political power has been a powerful impetus to the expansion of minority set-asides in municipal contracting. The superior performance of black emerging firms in large urban areas with presiding black mayors reflects the success of these preferential procurement efforts.

Such programs, however, must adapt to new judicial standards if they are to survive at the state and local government levels. Richmond, Virginia, had a minority business set-aside plan that required recipients of city-awarded construction contracts to subcontract at least 30 percent of each contract to minority-owned businesses. This set-aside law was challenged in court, culminating in the January 23, 1989, U.S. Supreme Court ruling (*Richmond* v. *Croson*) that it "violates the dictates of the Equal Protection Clause." Richmond argued that its law only attempted to remedy various forms of past discrimination, such as the exclusion of blacks from skilled construction trade unions and training programs. Writing for the majority, Supreme Court Justice Sandra O'Conner rejected this argument as "an amorphous claim." According to O'Conner, "a generalized assertion that there has been past discrimination in an entire industry provides no guidance for a legislative body to determine the precise scope of the injury it seeks to remedy." Despite the Court's negative ruling, O'Conner directly indicated that minority business set-aside programs in general may be found acceptable. "Nothing we say today," she wrote, "precludes a state or local entity from taking action to rectify the effects of identified discrimination within its jurisdiction." Furthermore, "evidence of a pattern of individual discriminatory acts can, if supported by appropriate statistical proof, lend support to a local government's determination that broader remedial relief is justified." Finally, where there is a significant statistical disparity between the number of qualified minority contractors willing and able to perform a particular service and the number of contractors actually engaged by the locality or its prime contractors, an inference of discriminatory exclusion could arise.

The references to "statistical proof" and "significant statistical disparity" make it clear that detailed, hard data on applicable business characteristics and practices will be required if government set-asides for minority business are to survive. Those programs that do survive the current flood of litigation on the heels of *Richmond* v. *Croson* are likely to have two traits: (1) detailed statistical documentation, and (2) vague language.

Detailed statistical documentation of discrimination. Many of the discriminatory practices that have shaped today's black business community appear to have been "ruled out" by the Supreme Court as possible justifications for preferential treatment of minority enterprise. Any serious student of racial discrimination knows, for example, that American Federation of Labor construction trade unions have often barred blacks from entering apprenticeship programs in the building trades. Mere common sense suggests that this discriminatory practice reduced the number of black-owned construction companies, particularly in trades such as plumbing, where discrimination was rampant.[1] Yet Justice O'Conner's majority opinion in *Croson* explicitly disregards the construction firms that *would have been* created by blacks discriminatorily excluded from apprentice programs. According to O'Conner, a disparity between the number of "qualified minority contractors willing and able to perform a particular service" and the number of such contractors "actually engaged by the locality" *could* lead to an inference of discrimination. But consider this hypothetical extreme case: no minority plumbing firms at all. In such a case there would be no qualified minority plumbers available "to perform a particular service" for the city; hence there would be no inference of discrimination by the city and no justification for an affirmative corrective measure. The *Croson* ruling is now the law of the land. Cities and states will presumably have to deal with it in coming years if they wish to pursue minority set-aside programs and so it is treated as a given in the discussion that follows.

In reality, states and large cities will probably be able to demonstrate statistically the necessary disparities between minority businesses' share of city (or state) contracts and the number of minority firms willing and able to undertake such work. Let us assume that, in a certain state, minority firms made up eight percent of all construction contractors. If, in fact, minority contractors had gotten only two percent of the dollar amount of all state-awarded construction work during the past decade, then the state government could legally adopt a goal of increasing the share of contracts targeted to minority firms. It would be a straightforward matter for this hypothetical state to select random samples of several hundred minority and nonminority contractors, and to survey them in order to establish scientifically the proportions of minority and nonminority contractors "willing and able" to work for the state.

The next step would be to turn these sample-based percentages into actual numbers. The U.S. Bureau of the Census produces reliable estimates of minority and nonminority firms, which could be used to establish the relative total numbers of minority and nonminority firms in most of the larger states. Such documentation of minority business underrepresentation would seem to fully meet the *Croson* ruling's strict scrutiny standard for justifying a minority business set-aside program. Among smaller states that have few minority firms—Delaware, New Hampshire, South Dakota, for example—federal databases are presently not capable of accurately describing the local minority business community. Statistical reliability simply cannot be achieved in geographic areas where minority businesses are scarce.

Nonetheless, it is perfectly feasible for many states and large cities to generate statistical proof of minority business underrepresentation in their share of procurement contract dollars, in the absence of set-aside programs. This type of detailed statistical documentation should indeed be compiled by cities and states that seriously desire to pursue these programs in coming years.

Another justification for minority set-asides that is likely to meet the Supreme Court's standard of strict scrutiny concerns the "passive participant" doctrine. According to Justice O'Conner, "Any public entity, state or federal, has a compelling interest in assuring that public dollars... do not serve to finance the evil of private prejudice.... [If] the city could show that it had essentially become a 'passive participant' in a system of racial exclusion... the city could take affirmative steps to dismantle such a system."

This book has documented that commercial banks today continue to redline black-owned businesses in urban minority communities. This lending discrimination weakens the prospects of black firms in general and harms their ability to compete for procurement contracts in particular. A set-aside program that sought to assist firms operating in redlined areas would be able to cite the "passive participant" doctrine to justify its actions.

Alternatively, cities could try to outlaw commercial bank redlining. In the end, however, they would lack the legal authority to enforce such laws. Cities do not charter banks, and it is unlikely that banks would willingly hand over the internal loan data cities would need to prove the practice of redlining. Moreover, very large international banks, such as Citicorp and Bank of America, operate in ways that make it difficult for federal regulatory agencies to keep tabs on them. The thought that New York City might effectively regulate any aspect of Citibank's operations is naive. What New York could do, however, is target business assistance to black entrepreneurs operating in redlined areas; in the absence of such assistance, the city would indeed be a passive participant in banks' discriminatory practices.

Vague language. Given the current legal climate, the set-aside programs that survive will no longer be referred to explicitly as minority business set-aside programs. Set-aside regulations will most likely refer to "disadvantaged" businesses, and government procurement officials will have broad discretionary powers to decide which firms qualify as disadvantaged. Perhaps the oldest of the large minority business set-aside efforts has been the federal Small Business Administration's 8(a) procurement program. Under 8(a), disadvantaged businesses are usually minority-owned; a report from SBA indicated that 96 percent of the 8(a) companies were owned by minorities. Yet the 8(a) effort is strictly a de facto minority business set-aside. It is altogether possible that procurement officials may in the future choose to shift 8(a) contracts away from minorities and toward low-income or women entrepreneurs.

Future minority business set-asides are likely to be based upon "goals" rather than rigid percentage requirements or quotas. Richmond, Virginia's now unconstitutional Minority Business Utilization Plan had required that prime construction contractors hired by the city subcontract at least 30 percent of each award to minority-owned businesses. A rewording of this law in the post-*Croson* era would refer to a *flexible goal* for subcontracting to disadvantaged businesses.

The goal is not only likely to be flexible, but may also be subject to waiver in the event that suitable disadvantaged businesses are unavailable. In the Supreme Court decision *Fullilove* v. *Klutznick,* which upheld federal minority set-asides, Justice Louis Powell stressed the "flexible waiver provisions" of the set-aside contained in the Public Works Employment Act of 1977. The Supreme Court's decision to uphold that program was partly based on this flexibility.

Of course, flexible programs that rely on goals for assisting disadvantaged businesses can only be effective if they are administered by committed officials. Vague wording of set-aside regulations necessarily puts great discretionary power into administrators' hands. This is not a new phenomenon. Procurement officials in some localities have been using their discretionary powers to water down the effectiveness of minority business set-asides for years.[2] This is one of the key reasons why black-owned businesses were observed (in chapter six) to be much more successful if they were located in areas with presiding black mayors. The presence of a black mayor highly correlates with the appointment of procurement officials who really do want to assist minority enterprises. The political will to make minority set-asides work effectively has always been vital to their success.

The Future of Set-Asides

Despite judicial challenges, it is possible that minority business assistance efforts will continue to expand in the years ahead. Programs to encourage minority business formation and growth continue to enjoy broad-based political support. It is instructive that the three major challenges to minority business assistance programs in the 1980s have not attacked the rationale for these programs. Rather, attacks have been aimed at the programs' effectiveness and legality.

Reports by the General Accounting Office as well as scholarly studies have documented inefficiencies in specific government efforts, such as SBA's embattled 8(a) procurement program. One of the complaints has been that a handful of politically well-connected minority enterprises—such as Wedtech Inc.—have benefited disproportionately from the 8(a) program.[3] In the case of Wedtech, prominent government officials, including congressmen and the U.S. attorney general, had lobbied to obtain defense department contracts for the firm. A small group of 8(a) firms has received the bulk of the SBA's 8(a) contract dollars. Of the many thousands of 8(a) firms, 31 percent of the contract-dollar volume accrued to a mere 50 firms, according to the General Accounting Office. According to the chief of the SBA's requirements division, successful 8(a) firms "have strong political connections that they are quick to use if any of their contracts are in jeopardy."[4]

Focusing upon another aspect of program effectiveness, the U.S. Commission on Civil Rights asserted in its 1986 report that government efforts to help minority business should be eliminated because they had not helped minority communities, "particularly in regard to increasing minority employment."[5] The Commission's report was seriously flawed, however; it presented no evidence to justify its strongly stated conclusion regarding the employment impact of minority business.

The Supreme Court's *Croson* ruling is the most far-reaching of the various challenges minority business-assistance programs have faced. The tension between the Fourteenth Amendment's guarantee of equal treatment to all citizens and the use of race-based measures to ameliorate the effects of discrimination was squarely addressed in this ruling, and it was resolved to the detriment of minority groups.

The line of criticism that focuses on program inefficiencies, by contrast, does not appear to threaten minority business assistance. While the SBA's Economic Opportunity Loan program, which assisted minority businesses largely but not exclusively, was abolished after its general ineffectiveness was repeatedly documented,[6] the more successful programs, such as SBA's 7(a) minority loan effort, are still in existence. In the realm of minority business set-asides, criticisms of program inefficiency have, to date, generated program reform rather than abolition.[7]

The superficial efforts of the U.S. Commission on Civil Rights to attack minority business assistance had little impact, in part because their criticisms were invalid. Chapter five of this volume documented that black firms operating in large urban areas employ a labor force that consists overwhelmingly of minority employees. In contrast, white-owned firms frequently use no minority workers, even when these firms are located in predominantly minority inner-city communities. Previous studies using nationwide data have reached similar conclusions about the employment patterns of black- versus white-owned businesses.[8] The evidence conclusively shows that an expanding black business community generates jobs for minority workers.

It must be kept in mind, finally, that while minority business programs may continue to enjoy broad-based political support, judicial support for many of these programs is problematic.

Combating Redlining: Opening Access to Financial Capital

The availability of commercial bank credit is a key problem for black business development. Chapters three and five of this study documented discriminatory loan treatment at the point of business startup, particularly for firms operating in urban minority communities. While information about bank lending to black firms after the startup stage was not available from the CBO database, the Ando study (discussed in chapters four and five) demonstrated that established black-owned businesses have far less access to commercial bank credit than their nonminority counterparts.

The constraint on financial capital available to black-owned businesses is unlikely to ease anytime soon. The low net-worth holdings that typify most black households will be alleviated, at best, only gradually over a period of many years. Limited personal wealth restricts business development in several ways. Commercial banks lend most freely to those who possess solid equity capital to invest in their businesses. Beyond banks, the second and third most important sources of loans for new small business are family and friends, respectively. The low net-worth holdings of black households in general mean, of course, that family and friends of black entrepreneurs are equally unlikely to be able to invest significantly in small business ventures.

In theory, the Community Reinvestment Act (CRA) of 1977 appears to address the problem of bank credit in urban minority neighborhoods. This act requires banks to service the borrowing needs of their local communities, including low-income areas such as inner-city minority neighborhoods. In fact, the applicable federal regulatory authorities have made no systematic attempts to define such abstract concepts as "the banking needs" of these communities. Likewise, no comprehensive attempts have been made to determine which banks are or are not meeting such needs.

Recent amendments to the CRA require that banks increase their collection of data regarding the race, sex, and income levels of their loan applicants and recipients. Further, bank regulatory agencies are now required to disclose information on the efforts of individual banks to service the credit needs of minority borrowers. The Community Reinvestment Act may therefore be a useful tool in the 1990s for prodding banks that are reluctant to finance minority borrowers.

If federal inaction continues despite ostensible strengthening of the CRA, state and local governments will need to enter the void to address the problem of commercial bank redlining. While cities have little power to measure, much less punish, redlining, the larger cities can exert some leverage on the banks. At the least, city governments can restrict their own banking business solely to those institutions with a record of actively lending in inner-city minority neighborhoods. Similarly, cities can publicize what they do know about bank lending patterns and call attention to those institutions that are least active in financing minority borrowers.

States can successfully demand information from banks on their lending practices. It is the states, after all, that charter many of the commercial banking institutions. If they care to, states can also outlaw discriminatory lending, and they can back up these laws with nontrivial sanctions. Banks that redline can be barred from opening new branches. They can be denied state government banking business. Redlining institutions can be barred from taking over other commercial banks, both intrastate as well as interstate. Banks rely upon public deposits as their primary source of funds and they are therefore sensitive to publicity regarding their good citizenship or the lack thereof. By focusing public scrutiny on the activities of redlining banks, cities and states have a powerful tool for encouraging nondiscriminatory bank lending practices. To date this tool has been underutilized.

Encouraging Business Development in Inner-City Minority Communities

An effective strategy for developing the ghetto's economy would have to include (1) developing lines of business that can employ the ghetto's supply of underutilized labor, and (2) relying heavily upon nonghetto sources for both capital and markets. Fundamental changes must take place in the flow of ghetto resources. To date, the majority of black-owned businesses exclusively serve a ghetto clientele. The activity of those businesses can only aid economic development, however, when other forces have generated rising incomes for ghetto residents. If black-owned businesses as a group rely solely upon the limited ghetto market, they will never achieve the economic strength necessary to alleviate inner-city problems.

The following example illustrates how the dynamics of resource inflows can benefit the overall ghetto economy. Assume that black firms in fields such as construction and manufacturing succeed in attracting large-scale procurement contracts from corporate and government sources. Assume, furthermore, that these contracts increase both the wage earnings of ghetto workers and the profits of the contract recipients. In this situation, black firms have successfully increased the flow of income into the ghetto, a portion of which will be spent through consumption at local retail and service establishments. The contract-holding firms will presumably use a portion of this income flow to purchase intermediate goods from local suppliers. Finally, part of the income flow will end up in local banks in checking and savings accounts. The spending and saving activities resulting from the initial income flow will generate a second round of spending and saving within the ghetto, causing what is known as the multiplier effect. The strength of the ensuing movement of income directly depends on the degree to which the recipient firms (and their employees) shop within the inner city: with more locally owned firms there is more rechanneling of funds and more respending within the local economy. As the multiplier effect strengthens, the resultant impact on ghetto incomes and employment also increases.

Note, however, that the streams of spending and responding percolating through the local economy are, in this example, entirely dependent on the income initially received by the black-owned construction and manufacturing firms from the outside economy: no inflow—no multiplier effect. Most of the ghetto's business community is ghetto-oriented and therefore fundamentally reactive to income flows influenced from outside. By contrast, ghetto businesses that can compete in the broader marketplace can actually shape the flow of income into the local economy. Further, the prospects of such firms are not held hostage by income levels within the ghetto, but depend instead on the firms' ability to compete in the broader economy. Yet powerful forces that currently dominate in the ghetto tend to undermine the development of such viable firms. Among these forces are weak internal markets, lack of capital, and an exodus of well-educated people.

Black-owned firms operating outside of minority communities assist ghetto areas in one very important respect—they create jobs for minority workers. But job creation is only one aspect of ghetto economic development. Other important aspects include strengthening local multiplier effects and investing capital inside the minority community. The strategy whereby a ghetto-based black business community would contribute directly and powerfully to local economic development is straightforward (in theory): businesses providing inner-city jobs would obtain outside capital to produce for outside markets. The practical questions raised by this strategy are similarly straightforward: who will provide the capital and the markets, and at what cost? Successful black-owned businesses have gravitated away from the inner city precisely because local ghetto markets are weak and financial capital is hard to raise. Enterprise zones could have the potential to lure these firms back into the inner city.

Enterprise zones. Former President Ronald Reagan endorsed "enterprise zones" as a tool for revitalizing business investment in depressed areas such as ghettos. The Reagan version of enterprise zones envisioned few government regulations, low taxes, and high levels of entrepreneurial initiative—supply-side economics for the ghetto. In practice, the aim of "few regulations" was never politically feasible: occupational safety and health rules, environmental restrictions, equal employment opportunity laws, and so forth remain intact in all versions of enterprise zone legislation. The Reagan program, in fact, based its incentives largely upon reducing capital gains taxes, a technique that is particularly unsuited for generating jobs for local residents.[9]

Taxes are one of the less important considerations when deciding where to locate a business, and urban enterprise zones would have to compete with a variety of tax concessions that many states and cities offer to attract business investment. Tax concessions alone will not lure the business investment required to revitalize ghetto economies: they provide very little in the way of financial capital to fund business startups, and they provide even less in the way of markets to absorb the new businesses' output.

Upgrading the local infrastructure, on the other hand, is essential if the urban enterprise zone strategy is to become viable. Reagan's enterprise zone concept of "unfettered free enterprise" notwithstanding, what is in fact needed is a concentrated public investment in the ghetto's infrastructure: public service improvement, land use planning, business loan funds, and access to outside markets.

One state-sponsored enterprise zone, in Louisville, Kentucky—though it is too recent to be properly evaluated— shows strong promise. Louisville's effort is an excellent example of how a whole set of policies can be coordinated to make enterprise zones work for minority residents as well as for business owners. The city's enterprise zone covers 2,400 acres of land, including (1) 12,000 residents, (2) old industrial buildings suitable for rehabilitation, (3) vacant land, and (4) ongoing businesses. The zone is surrounded by low-income residential areas. It also has easy access to two interstate highways and three railroad lines. The city has spent or committed more than $50 million to land clearance and assembly as well as infrastructure development, aimed largely at making the industrial areas more attractive to potential business investment. Working with local banks, Louisville is developing a pool of $30 million in financing for firms that locate within the zone. Added to these incentives are reductions in utility fees, connection charges, and various state and local taxes. To be eligible for all these benefits, firms investing in the zone must employ at least 25 percent of their workers from local residents having "disadvantaged" backgrounds (which includes zone residents, unemployed persons, public assistance recipients, and so forth).[10]

Louisville's enterprise zone addresses some of the most fundamental needs of the urban ghetto: it could reverse the drain of resources that maintains ghetto poverty. Together with the ghetto's chief resource—its labor—this strategy could raise many in the ghetto out of poverty and start a self-generating process of economic development.

At this stage, we do not know how well the Louisville program is working. Relative to the costs of investing in infrastructure, improving public services, and subsidizing loans to enterprise-zone businesses, how many successful business startups and expansions have been generated? Of the resultant jobs created, how many have gone to minority workers? Are net new jobs being created, or is employment simply being shifted to the enterprise zone from other parts of Louisville? A comprehensive accounting of the benefits and the costs produced by the various enterprise zone efforts throughout the country is vitally needed. Enterprise zones of the future must learn from the successes and failures of existing efforts.

The participation of black-owned businesses in enterprise zones would certainly be furthered by making debt capital more readily available to promising firms. Inventive political leaders in local government have potentially powerful development tools at their disposal. Development capital could be channeled into the inner city, for example, by depositing city and state government funds in local banks on the condition that the banks lend actively to enterprise-zone firms. Furthermore, city and state funds could be used either to guarantee such bank loans (in the event of default) or to participate directly with banks in appropriate business financing. Similarly, the procurement powers of local government could be used to provide markets for enterprise-zone firms, just as set-aside programs are now utilized to provide markets for minority-owned businesses in general. Strategies for generating inner-city economic development should ultimately be chosen though the trial-and-error process of identifying cost-effective methods for sustaining businesses that generate employment.

Strong political leadership, political cohesiveness, and local political control could make it possible to institute such a development program. The election of black officials alone cannot solve the ghetto's problems. It is important that an ambitious program, one that attacks the very roots of ghetto poverty, be produced. Such a program is necessary as well to mobilize political support within the inner-city minority community and to build the economic foundations for sustained political action.

Appendix A: The Characteristics of Business Owners Database

S amples of business owners analyzed in chapters two through six are drawn most frequently from the 1982 Characteristics of Business Owners (CBO) survey. This survey was compiled by the U.S. Bureau of the Census in 1987. The CBO database is the first database of national scope that both describes self-employed people as individuals and describes the traits of the businesses they own, such as sales, earnings, employees, and capital inputs. The CBO survey drew its sample from business owners who responded to the 1982 Survey of Minority-Owned Business Enterprises or the 1982 Survey of Women-Owned Businesses. These two surveys were drawn from the universe of persons who filed one of the following types of federal income tax forms in 1982: (1) Schedule C, Form 1040 (sole proprietorships); (2) Form 1065 (owners of partnerships); or (3) Form 1120-S (owners of subchapter S business corporations) (U.S. Department of Commerce, Bureau of the Census, 1987).

The CBO survey form was sent out to 125,000 self-employed individuals in 1986. By design, women and minorities were overrepresented: subsamples of 25,000 blacks, 25,000 Hispanics, 25,000 women, and 25,000 other minorities (Asians, primarily) made up the bulk of the CBO survey universe. One additional noteworthy aspect of the CBO database is the fact that the survey response rate was

81 percent overall. This very high response rate is unusual in the realm of business surveys.

A problem is presented by the fact that many who file tax returns such as Schedule C are operating "casual" businesses. Among persons filing Schedule C forms, many are therefore not small business owners according to the commonly understood meaning of the term. Quite frequently, these casual business operators have invested no financial capital in their "firms." These business operators —typically employees who have periodic self-employment income—are largely excluded from this book by the imposition of two restrictive criteria. For the purposes of this study, small business firms are defined as the subset of the CBO sample for which: (1) financial capital investment in the business is greater than zero, and (2) annual sales in 1982 were at least $5,000. Applying these restrictions reduces the CBO samples of firms by more than 50 percent. The CBO data selected for this study are therefore representative—regarding industry mix and geographic location—of small business proprietorships, partnerships, and small business corporations that file tax returns.

The CBO survey's focus on individual owners led to editing problems in cases where firms had more than one owner. This was handled by editing the data so that each firm appears only once in the analysis files. In the case of a firm with five owners, for example, the first owner who responded to the survey—specifically, the owner with the lowest census file number—would be selected. This is equivalent to randomly selecting one of the responding owners; a hypothetical nonrespondent would have no chance of being selected. A new variable would be created by taking the sum of the financial capital (debt and equity) contributed by all five owners: this variable measures a firm's total financial capital. This information would be added to the record of the first owner; then the other four owners would be dropped from further consideration. The resultant database is introduced in chapter two's analysis of traditional black businesses, and it is examined extensively throughout this book.

Appendix B: Summary Tables and Econometric Models for Chapter Three

This appendix presents three tables of summary statistics (tables B.1, B.2, and B.4) discussed in chapter three. It also summarizes the results of three econometric modeling exercises. Linear regression models are used to explain 1982 total sales levels for black- and white-owned firms (table B.3) and to explain the levels of debt capital input for firms that received commercial bank loans as groups of black and white loan recipients are analyzed separately (table B.5). A discriminant analysis model is used to differentiate between active black firms and those that have discontinued operations (table B.6).

All of the variables used in these three separate econometric exercises are defined below. Note that certain variables are used in every econometric model, while other variables may appear in only one of the models. All of the applicable variables are drawn from the CB0 data source described in appendix A. Variables utilized in the econometric exercises include explicit measures of owner human capital as well as (1) year of entry into self-employment, (2) age and sex of owner, and (3) whether the owner created a firm from scratch or acquired an existing business. The CB0 survey collected data on the amounts of financial capital used by self-employed persons to start or become owners of their businesses; these include variables measuring total financial inputs at the point of business entry as well as the component parts, debt capital and equity capital. Other relevant variables include (1) average hours of labor contributed per week by the business owner, (2) the industry of the business, (3) 1982 sales volume, and (4) whether or not the business was still operating in late 1986. Businesses still operating in 1986 are referred to as "active" firms; those that have closed down are "discontinued." Exact variable definitions are summarized below.

Education

Ed2: For owners completing four years of high school, the value of Ed2 = 1; otherwise Ed2 = 0.

Ed3: For owners completing at least one but less than four years of college, the value of Ed3 = 1; otherwise Ed3 = 0.

Ed4: For owners completing four or more years of college, the value of Ed4 = 1; otherwise Ed4 = 0.

Management Experience

For owners who had worked in a managerial capacity prior to owning the business they owned in 1982, *Management* = the number of years one had worked as a manager.

Age and Sex of Owner

Age2: For owners between the ages of 35 and 44, Age2 = 1 ; otherwise Age2 = 0.

Age3: For owners between the ages of 45 and 54, Age3 = 1 ; otherwise Age3 = 0.

Age4: For owners 55 or older, Age4 = 1 ; otherwise Age4 = 0.

Sex: For male owners, Sex = 1 ; otherwise, Sex = 0.

Labor Input and Firm Acquisition

Labor input: The average number of hours per week in 1982 spent by the owner working in or managing the business that he/she owned.

126

Ongoing: If the owner entered a business that was already in operation, Ongoing = 1 ; if the owner was the original founder of the business, then Ongoing = 0.

Year of Firm Startup

For the year in which the business was started or acquired two variables reflect the following categories:

Time82: If the business was started or ownership was acquired during 1982, then Time82 = 1; otherwise Time82 = 0.

Time80: If the business was started or ownership was acquired during 1980 or 1981, then Time80 = 1 ; otherwise Time80 = 0.

Debt, Equity, Leverage, and Related Variables

Debt is defined as borrowed money used to start or become an owner of the business, measured in dollars.

Equity is defined as financial capital (other than borrowed money) used to start or become an owner of the business, measured in dollars. The dollar value of business assets contributed by the owner at the point of business entry is also included as equity.

Leverage: The ratio of debt to equity; the value of this ratio is constrained not to exceed 19.

Log Capital: The logarithm of the sum of debt and equity capital.

Log Sales: The logarithm of total sales revenues for the 1982 calendar year.

Industry Groupings

A series of self-explanatory dummy variables is employed to identify firms in six major industry groups: (1) *Construction*, (2) *Manufacture*, (3) *Transportation* (includes communication and public utilities), (4) *Trade* (includes both wholesale and retail industries), (5) *FIRE* (includes finance, insurance, and real estate), and (6) *Service.*

In the econometric exercises summarized in tables B.3, B.5, and B.6 of this appendix, no education variable is used to measure the presence (or absence) of owners having less than 12 years of formal schooling; the age variables similarly contain no direct measure of owners under age 35.

The technical details of the econometric models estimated in this chapter are described in a fashion that is appropriate for a readership of nonspecialists. Much more detailed technical discussions—regarding hypothesized relationships, variable function form, and choice of econometric technique—are readily available (see Bates 1990a).

Table B.1
Selected Statistics: Firms by Employer Status—Employers Versus Firms Having No Employees

	Black-Owned Businesses Only			White Male Businesses Only		
	All	Employer firms	Zero employee firms	All	Employer firms	Zero employee firms
Business Traits (mean value)						
Total sales, 1982	$55,402	$138,030	$28,421	$164,003	$378,549	$47,268
No. employees, 1982	0.8	3.0	NA	2.0	5.6	NA
Owner Traits						
Total financial capital (mean)*	$15,908	$28,095	$11,929	$37,170	$60,950	$24,244
Equity capital (mean)	$7,945	$12,346	$6,509	$17,815	$28,626	$11,932
Debt capital (mean)	$7,963	$15,749	$5,420	$19,363	$32,324	$12,321
Percent with under 4 years of high school	25.5%	22.5%	26.4%	15.4%	12.9%	16.8%
Percent with 4 or more years of college	24.5%	29.0%	23.0%	32.9%	37.5%	30.3%
Percent of Firms Still in Business, 1986	75.1%	82.0%	72.9%	78.0%	84.7%	74.3%
(N=)	4,883	1,202	3,681	7,807	2,751	5,056

*At the date of entry into self-employment ($ figures are not inflation-adjusted).

Table B.2
Business Characteristics by Age of Firm

	Black-Owned Businesses Only			White Male Businesses Only		
	All firms	Firms formed before 1976	Firms formed 1976–1982	All firms	Firms formed before 1976	Firms formed 1976–1982
Business Traits (mean value)						
Total sales, 1982	$55,402	$66,788	$47,184	$164,003	$223,280	$118,790
No. employees, 1982	0.8	1.0	0.6	2.0	2.7	1.5
Owner Traits						
Total financial capital (mean)*	$15,908	$11,534	$19,066	$32,178	$27,510	$44,552
Equity capital (mean)*	$7,945	$6,411	$9,054	$17,815	$14,423	$20,402
Debt capital (mean)*	$7,963	$5,123	$10,012	$19,363	$13,088	$24,150
Percent with under 4 years of high school	25.5%	35.0%	18.5%	15.4%	20.8%	11.3%
Percent with 4 or more years of college	24.5%	18.9%	28.5%	32.9%	29.6%	35.3%
Percent of Firms Still in Business, 1986	75.1%	83.2%	71.0%	78.0%	83.2%	74.0%
(N=)	4,883	2,047	2,836	7,807	3,378	4,429

*At the date of entry into self-employment (dollar figures are not inflation-adjusted).

Table B.3
Linear Regression Models: Explaining 1982 Total Sales for Firms Entered in the 1976–1981 Time Period

	Black Firms Only		White Firms Only	
	Regression coefficient	Standard error	Regression coefficient	Standard error
Constant	6.512*	0.183	7.150*	0.304
Labor input	0.011*	0.001	0.013*	0.001
Ed2	0.144*	0.064	0.062	0.066
Ed3	0.064	0.068	0.034	0.071
Ed4	0.149*	0.075	0.209*	0.076
Management	0.000	0.004	0.010*	0.003
Log capital	0.313*	0.018	0.337*	0.014
Age2	0.139*	0.063	- 0.006	0.047
Age3	0.106*	0.056	- 0.049	0.058
Age4	0.037	0.076	- 0.223*	0.071
Ongoing	0.075	0.074	0.290*	0.046
Time80	- 0.167*	0.042	- 0.258*	0.038
Manufacture	- 0.014	0.168	0.426*	0.086
Construction	0.396*	0.111	0.293*	0.078
Transportation	0.065	0.099	0.042	0.084
Trade	0.421*	0.083	0.576*	0.069
FIRE	- 0.196	0.134	- 0.041	0.091
Services	- 0.024	0.080	0.203*	0.066
(N=)	2,155		3,657	
(R²=)	0.254		0.281	
(F=)	38.27		74.89	

*Statistically significant at the alpha = .05 level.

Note: The dependent variable in the above regression equations is the logarithm of 1982 total sales.

Table B.4
Financial Capital Structure of Borrowers:
Firms Entered in the Period 1976–1982

	Black Firms	White Male Firms
A. All CBO Sample Firms With Debt Capital Input Greater Than Zero		
Total financial capital at time of entry		
Mean	$32,813	$70,756
Median	$7,500	$17,500
Percent under $10,000	52.3%	30.9%
Percent under $50,000	87.9%	73.2%
Equity		
Mean	$10,734	$22,071
Median	$2,625	$4,250
Percent under $5,000	66.3%	51.9%
Debt		
Mean	$22,079	$48,684
Median	$5,625	$14,875
Percent under $5,000	49.2%	28.3%
Leverage* (mean)	6.39	7.25
(N=)	(1,286)	(2,197)
B. Bank Loan Recipients Only		
Total financial capital at time of entry		
Mean	$36,530	$76,318
Median	$15,000	$22,500
Percent under $10,000	47.2%	27.7%
Percent under $50,000	86.6%	71.7%
Equity		
Mean	$10,826	$20,514
Median	$2,625	$4,375
Percent under $5,000	66.1%	52.8%
Debt		
Mean	$25,704	$55,803
Median	$7,125	$16,625
Percent under $5,000	43.1%	24.6%
Leverage* (mean)	6.33	7.89
Percent of sample** with bank loans	55.5%	64.6%
(N=)	(714)	(1,419)

*Leverage is defined as the ratio of debt to equity; it is constrained so that the value of the ratio cannot exceed 19. This constraint is internal in the data base and, therefore, it cannot be altered or relaxed.
**Includes borrowers only.

Table B.5
Linear Regression Models: Explaining Debt Capital Inputs for Commercial Bank Loan Recipients (Only) Entering Business in the Period 1976–1982

	White Firms Only		Black Firms Only	
	Regression coefficient	Standard error	Regression coefficient	Standard error
Constant	-8,261.060	12,118.279	14,386.918	10,834.467
Ed2	16,378.546	12,085.385	-2,151.482	10,355.462
Ed3	14,783.465	13,308.299	-13,375.310	11,107.711
Ed4	28,552.929*	12,363.037	27,110.584*	10,601.726
Management	-182.427	589.858	326.059	648.300
Equity capital	1.835*	0.042	1.164*	0.085
Age2	10,433.854	9,179.578	-8,963.618	9,101.468
Age3	4,869.243	11,003.469	-13,736.249	10,360.929
Age4	12,095.686	14,865.736	-14,487.144	13,533.935
Ongoing	14,127.628*	8,193.540	7,863.444	8,260.903
(N=)	1,419		714	
(R²=)	0.585		0.238	
(F=)	220.390		24.410	

*Statistically significant at the alpha = .05 level.

Note: The dependent variable in the above regression equations is the dollar amount of debt capital invested at the point of business startup.

Table B.6
Discriminant Analysis: Blacks Entering Business in the Period 1976–1982

	Discriminant Function Standardized Coefficients	Group Mean Vectors	
		Active firms	Discontinued firms
Ed2	-0.034	0.284	0.293
Ed3	-0.030	0.236	0.255
Ed4	0.114	0.289	0.277
Labor input	0.169	41.924	38.812
Management	-0.116	3.725	3.753
Age2	0.094	0.358	0.359
Age3	0.275	0.273	0.225
Age4	0.021	0.123	0.125
Sex	0.104	0.763	0.723
Leverage	0.181	3.142	2.353
Log Capital	0.404	8.827	8.577
Ongoing	-0.291	0.219	0.270
Time80	-0.614	0.353	0.417
Time82	-0.705	0.215	0.297
(N=)		1,963	873

Wilk's lamba statistic = 0.961.
F = 7.56: the group differences are statistically significant (alpha = .01 level).

Appendix C: Summary Tables and Econometric Models for Chapter Five

This appendix, which presents two tables of summary statistics described in chapter five, summarizes the results of two econometric modeling exercises:

First, linear regression models are used to explain debt capital input levels for groups of black and white firms in 28 SMSAs that received commercial bank loans. As in the analyses for chapter three, the black and white firm groups are analyzed separately (table C.2).

Second, discriminant analysis models are used to differentiate between active firms and those that have discontinued operations. Three groups of firms are analyzed separately: (1) black firms located in minority neighborhoods of 28 SMSAs (table C.3); (2) black firms located in nonminority areas of 28 SMSAs (table C.3); and (3) white firms located in the 28 SMSAs (table C.4).

All of the variables used in these econometric exercises are defined in Appendix B. As in the chapter three econometric exercises, the education variable group excludes owners having less than 12 years of formal schooling, while the age group excludes owners under age 35.

Table C.1
Business Characteristics of Firms Operating In Large Metropolitan Areas

	All Businesses		Employers Only	
	Black firms	White male firms	Black firms	White male firms
Business Traits				
Total sales, 1982	$56,342	$166,762	$153,116	$393,806
No. of employees, 1982	0.7	2.0	3.0	5.8
Owner Traits				
Total financial capital* (mean)	$16,059	$37,314	$28,204	$63,937
Equity capital* (mean)	$8,448	$20,867	$13,090	$34,532
Debt capital* (mean)	$7,611	$16,447	$15,114	$29,405
Percent with under 4 years of high school	29.9%	13.0%	18.6%	12.5%
Percent with 4 or more years of college	27.3%	41.0%	30.8%	42.5%
Percent of Firms Still in Business, 1986	73.9%	78.1%	82.4%	85.4%
(N=)	2,318	1,815	533	630

Source: CBO survey data (unpublished); sample selection is described in chapter one.

*At the date of entry into self-employment (dollar figures are not inflation-adjusted).

Table C.2
Linear Regression Models Explaining Debt Capital Inputs for Firms Entering Business in the 1976–1982 Time Period: Firms Operating in Large Metropolitan Areas

	Black Firms		White Firms	
	Regression coefficient	Standard error	Regression coefficient	Standard error
Constant	47,286.875	38,527.746	-25,963.528	28,177.383
Ed2	-5,403.068	28,085.396	30,827.339	29,727.324
Ed3	-26,044.350	29,714.531	221.711	30,615.072
Ed4	38,628.402**	28,606.126	34,109.655	28,118.250
Age2	-29,285.456	23,153.396	-4,829.869	18,612.486
Age3	-32,657.423	26,390.336	-5,279.664	23,041.707
Age4	-24,641.492	36,914.442	-24,204.688	28,442.568
Equity capital	0.893*	0.165	1.791*	0.224
Management	784.306	1,564.750	2,133.739*	1,207.081
Ongoing	24,769.583	20,177.228	49,995.605*	17,514.899
Minority area	-39,563.531*	18,117.158	-4,179.516	29,235.917
(N=)	271		248	
(R²=)	0.164		0.301	
(F=)	4.31		10.21	

*Statistically significant, alpha = .05

**Statistically significant, alpha = .10

Note: Debt and equity are measured in dollars.

Table C.3
Discriminant Analysis: Black Firms in Large SMSAs Entering Business in the Period 1976–1982

	1st Model: Firms in Minority Communities Only			2nd Model: Firms in Nonminority Communities Only		
	Discriminant Function Coefficients	Group Mean Vectors		Discriminant Function Coefficients	Group Mean Vectors	
	Standardized coefficients	Active firms	Discont. firms	Standardized coefficients	Active firms	Discont. firms
Ed2	-0.322	0.280	0.317	0.399	0.277	0.260
Ed3	-0.274	0.246	0.276	0.521	0.203	0.204
Ed4	-0.101	0.283	0.256	0.654	0.420	0.401
Management	-0.077	3.527	3.644	-0.099	4.022	3.923
Input	0.062	42.023	39.389	0.195	41.792	37.250
Age2	-0.228	0.335	0.369	0.074	0.415	0.408
Age3	0.055	0.309	0.240	0.263	0.233	0.225
Age4	-0.354	0.114	0.154	0.217	0.111	0.056
Log Capital	0.324	8.759	8.539	0.341	8.893	8.643
Leverage	0.213	2.499	1.695	0.156	3.105	2.418
Ongoing	-0.436	0.206	0.292	-0.142	0.199	0.232
Minority market	0.224	0.657	0.596	—	—	—
Open market	—	—	—	0.075	0.559	0.515
Time80	-0.661	0.329	0.423	-0.620	0.416	0.472
Time82	-0.600	0.216	0.282	-0.858	0.199	0.330
Sex	0.004	0.741	0.724	-0.129	0.760	0.786
(N=)		621	321		296	142

Multivariate test for differences between the two groups:

1st Model: Wilk's lamba statistic = .937.
F= 4.07: the group differences are statistically significant at the alpha = .01 level.

2nd Model: Wilk's lamba statistic = .927.
F= 2.91: the group differences are statistically significant at the alpha = .01 level.

Table C.4
Discriminant Analysis: Whites Entering Business in the 1976–1982 Time Period

	Discriminant Function Coefficients	Group Mean Vectors	
	Standardized coefficients	Active firms	Discontinued firms
Ed2	-0.142	0.239	0.325
Ed3	0.211	0.219	0.214
Ed4	0.383	0.456	0.269
Management	-0.135	5.995	5.650
Input	0.249	44.881	42.537
Age2	0.025	0.338	0.329
Age3	0.095	0.196	0.182
Age4	0.185	0.134	0.111
Log Capital	0.405	9.375	9.018
Leverage	-0.210	2.375	3.211
Ongoing	0.251	0.230	0.159
Minority market	-0.211	0.087	0.119
Time80	-0.539	0.397	0.472
Time82	-0.651	0.154	0.238
Minority area	-0.075	0.157	0.170
(N=)		766	252

Multivariate test for differences between the two groups:

Wilk's lamba statistic = .948.
F = 4.63: the group differences are statistically significant at the alpha = .01 level.

Table C.5
The Incidence of Minority Employees on the Payrolls of White and Black-Owned Firms (Includes firms located in 28 large metropolitan areas only)

A. All Employers:

Percent minority employees	Black Firms	White Firms
75 percent or more	89.0%	17.8%
50 percent or more	93.5	23.2
Fewer than 50 percent (but greater than zero)	4.3	19.0
No minority employees	2.2	57.8

B. Employers by Area:

Percent minority employees	Firms Located in Minority Neighborhoods		Firms Located in Nonminority Areas	
	Black Firms	White Firms	Black Firms	White Firms
75 percent or more	93.1%	29.4%	78.9%	15.5%
50 percent or more	96.2	37.6	86.7	20.4
Fewer than 50 percent (but greater than zero)	1.9	29.4	10.2	16.9
No minority employees	1.9	32.9	3.1	62.7
Percent of employers located in each type of geographic area	71.3	16.4	28.7	83.6

Notes

Notes to Chapter 1

1. Jaynes and Williams, 1989.

2. Danziger and Gottschalk, 1986.

3. Jaynes and Williams, 1989, p. 17.

4. *Ibid.*, p. 375.

5. *Ibid.*, p. 306.

6. *Ibid.*, p. 289.

7. *Ibid.*, p. 26.

8. *Ibid.*, p. 323.

9. Ledebur and Garn, 1980.

10. Vaughn, 1983.

11. Bates and Fusfeld, 1984, ch. 8,9; Harrison and Bluestone, 1985.

12. Birch, 1987, p. 16.

13. Armington and Odle, 1982; Harris, 1983.

14. Bates and Fusfeld 1984.

15. *Ibid.*, ch. 9.

16. Bates and Fusfeld, 1984.

17. In their recent study of South Carolina textile firms, for example, Heckman and Payner (1989) demonstrate that federal government equal-opportunity efforts were major factors in the large increase in black employment during the 1960s in an industry that had previously barred almost all black workers.

18. Jaynes and Williams, 1989, p. 321.

19. Braddock and McPartland, 1987, p. 12.

20. Tabb, 1972; Osborne and Granfield, 1976; Bates and Bradford, 1979; U.S. Commission on Civil Rights, 1986.

21. Stevens, 1984; U.S. Bureau of the Census, 1985.

22. Brimmer, 1966; Brimmer and Terrell, 1971.

23. Markwalder, 1983; Brimmer and Terrell, 1971.

24. Bates, 1981; 1983.

25. Simms, 1988.

Notes to Chapter 2

1. Bates and Grown, 1992.

2. Bates, 1989c; 1990c.

3. Holsey, 1938.

4. Kelsey, 1903.

5. Ransom and Sutch, 1977.

6. Bates and Fusfeld, 1984.

7. Bates, 1973b.

8. Pierce, 1947.

9. Bates, 1973b.

10. Watkins, 1985.

11. National Institute of Government Purchasing, 1984.

12. Bates, 1987.

13. Bates, 1989a.

14. I have excluded "casual" businesses—defined as those having 1982 annual sales of under $5,000—but CBO enterprise data are otherwise representative of the small business universe that existed in 1982.

15. Bates, 1987.

16. *Ibid.*

17. These findings emerged from earlier studies by the author based on 1960, 1970, and 1980 census data; see Bates, 1984; 1987; and 1988a.

Notes to Chapter 3

1. Bates, 1987.

2. See, for example, U.S. Census Bureau, *Survey of Minority-Owned Business Enterprises, 1975.*

3. Markwalder, 1981.

4. Bates and Nucci, 1989.

5. Bearse, 1983.

6. Bates, 1988a, pp. 31–5.

7. These figures on mean retail sales are based on CBO data, and they are comparable to the data summarized in table B.2 in appendix B.

8. Jovanovic, 1982.

9. Some readers may wonder why the term *discontinue* is used rather than the more familiar term *fail.* In fact, the government data on businesses which this book draws on are unable to distinguish between those firms that have closed because of failure to make a profit and those that have ended operation for family reasons or because of the owner's ill health, old age, or landing a more attractive job. All closings, then, are discontinuances, but only some are accurately labeled "failures."

10. This range of sales dispersion is measured as the coefficient of variation, that is, the standard deviation divided by the mean.

11. Bates, 1973a; Evans, 1987.

12. Jovanovic, 1982; Bates, 1989a.

13. Bates, 1990a.

14. Evans and Jovanovic, 1989; Bates, 1989a.

15. Holmes and Schmitz, 1990.

16. Terrell, 1971.

17. Jaynes and Williams, 1989, p. 292.

18. Bradford, 1988.

19. Statistical techniques for estimating small business size, such as table B.3's multiple regression technique, are not perfect predictors of firm behavior. For example, the variable for the hours of owner labor input suffers from a statistical problem known as "bi-direction of causality" when it is used to explain firm sales level. More labor input by owners, according to table B.3's statistical finding, indeed results in higher sales levels.

But consider the following hypothetical situation: an owner who pursues self-employment on a part-time basis finds that sales are booming in mid-1982. Because of this strength in business sales, the owner starts to work at the firm full-time. In this case, higher sales levels *cause* the owner to work longer hours in self-employment: by working longer hours, in turn, increased business sales levels are realized.

The regression analysis assumes that working longer hours (the independent variable) results in higher sales levels (the dependent variable); it does *not* measure the impact of dependent variable changes upon independent variable inputs (bi-direction of causality). For this reason, the statistical results (table B.3) must be viewed as being possibly biased. Such biases are the norm in cases where complex interactions exist between a variety of economic factors (such as owner traits) and the performance of an economic entity (such as small businesses). One response to such ubiquitous biases is to estimate several different econometric models that explain closely related dependent variables.

20. Bates, 1987.

21. Bates, 1974.

22. Brennan and Schwartz, 1978.

23. Bates and Hester, 1977.

24. Bates and Bradford, 1979.

Notes to Chapter 4

1. Bates, 1981.

2. Bates, 1985a.

3. Levinson, 1980.

4. Bates, 1981.

5. Handy and Swinton, 1984.

6. Bates and Fusfeld, 1984.

7. Ihlanfeldt and Sjoquist, 1990.

8. Jaynes and Williams, 1987, p. 321.

9. Anderson, 1980, 1986; Braddock and McPartland, 1987.

10. Jaynes and Williams, 1989, p. 322.

11. Oakland, Sparrow, and Stettler, 1971.

12. Schaffer, 1973.

13. The role of income drains in preserving ghetto poverty is comprehensively documented in Richard Schaffer's classic New York City study, *Income Flows in Urban Poverty Areas: A Comparison of the Community Income Accounts of Bedford-Stuyvesant and Borough Park* (1973).

14. Browne, 1971.

15. Schaffer, 1973.

16. Sternlieb and Burchell, 1973.

17. Ando, 1988; Bates and Bradford, 1979.

18. Bates and Bradford, 1979.

19. Boorman and Kwast, 1974.

20. Bates and Bradford, 1979.

21. Bates and Fusfeld, 1984.

Notes to Chapter 5

1. Ando, 1988.

2. Several urban areas, such as San Antonio and San Jose, had relatively few blacks in census tracts with those poverty rates and were therefore excluded from the study. Other large urban areas—e.g., San Diego and Seattle—were dropped because they lacked a sufficient number of high-poverty census tracts, while still others were dropped because they were too small and lacked a sufficient number of black-owned businesses.

3. Cited by Evans and Jovanovic, 1989.

4. Bates, 1983.

Notes to Chapter 6

1. Jaynes and Williams, 1989, p. 250.

2. Eisinger, 1984, p. 252.

3. Bates, 1985b.

4. Minority business directories utilized by corporate and government procurement officials were used in a 1983 study to generate names of minority firms that were actual or potential participants in set-aside

and preferential procurement programs. The minority business names thus extracted were matched against Dun and Bradstreet (D and B) files, and the matching process produced useful data on more than 1,000 minority firms (Bates, 1985b).

5.   Five of these areas dominate the analysis, because they contain nearly 83 percent of the applicable black business sample. These five dominant areas are Atlanta, Detroit, Los Angeles, Oakland, and Washington, D.C. Similarly, the 18 areas without black mayors in 1982 are dominated by seven regions that contain over 74 percent of the applicable black business sample; these are New York, Chicago, Houston, Philadelphia, Dallas, Baltimore, and St. Louis. The 10 areas—Atlanta to Washington, D.C.—are identified as the "black mayor" group in this study; the remaining 18 areas are the "other mayor" group.

Notes to Chapter 7

1.   Bates and Fusfeld, 1984, pp. 68–70.

2.   Methods used by state and local governments to circumvent the intent of minority business set-aside programs are described in numerous journalistic sources. See, for example, the *Wall Street Journal* ("States Say It's Not So Easy Finding Minority Concerns," April 3, 1985) and the *Chicago Tribune* ("51% Solution Creates Instant Minority Firms," June 9, 1985).

3.   Bates, 1985a.

4.   U.S. Comptroller General, 1981, p. 10.

5.   U.S. Commission on Civil Rights, 1986, p. 2.

6.   Bates and Bradford, 1979.

7.   Bates, 1985a.

8.   Bates, 1988b.

9.   Bendick and Rasmussen, 1986, pp. 105–18.

10.   Bendick and Rasmussen, 1986.

BIBLIOGRAPHY

Anderson, Elijah. 1980. "Some Observations on Black Youth Employment." In *Youth Employment Issues and Policy*, edited by Bernard Anderson and Isabel Sawhill (Englewood Cliffs, N.J.: Prentice-Hall).

_____. 1986. "Of Old Heads and Young Boys: Notes on the Urban Black Experience." Paper prepared for the National Research Council's Committee on the Status of Black Americans (Washington, D.C.).

Ando, Faith. 1988. *An Analysis of Access to Bank Credit*. Los Angeles: UCLA Center for Afro-American Studies.

Armington, C., and M. Odle. 1982. "Small Business: How Many Jobs?" *Brookings Review* (Winter).

Bates, Timothy. 1973a. "An Econometric Analysis of Lending to Black Businessmen." *The Review of Economics and Statistics* (August).

_____. 1973b. *Black Capitalism: A Quantitative Analysis*. New York: Praeger.

_____. 1974. "Financing Black Enterprise." *Journal of Finance* (June).

_____. 1981. "Black Entrepreneurship and Government Programs." *Journal of Contemporary Studies* (Fall).

_____. 1983. "Small Business Administration Loan Programs." In *Sources of Financing for Small Businesses*, edited by Paul Horvitz and R.R. Pettit (Greenwich, Connecticut: JAI Press).

_____. 1984. "An Analysis of the Minority Entrepreneur: Traits and Trends." Unpublished report to the U.S. Department of Commerce Minority Business Development Agency.

_____. 1985a. "Impact of Preferential Procurement Policies on Minority-Owned Business." *The Review of Black Political Economy* (Summer).

_____. 1985b. "Entrepreneur Human Capital Endowments and Minority Business Viability." *The Journal of Human Resources* (Fall).

_____. 1987. "Self-Employed Minorities: Traits and Trends." *Social Science Quarterly* (September).

_____. 1988a. *An Analysis of the Earnings Levels of Self-Employed Minorities*. Los Angeles: UCLA Center for Afro-American Studies.

_____. 1988b. "Do Black-Owned Businesses Employ Minority Workers? New Evidence." *The Review of Black Political Economy* (Spring).

_____. 1989a. "Small Business Viability in the Urban Ghetto." *Journal of Regional Science* (November).

_____. 1989b. "Entrepreneur Factor Inputs and Small Business Longevity." Working paper. U.S. Bureau of the Census Center for Economic Studies (July).

_____. 1989c. "The Changing Nature of Minority Business: A Comparative Analysis of Asian, Nonminority, and Black-Owned Businesses." *The Review of Black Political Economy* (Fall).

_____. 1990a. "Entrepreneur Human Capital Inputs and Small Business Longevity." *The Review of Economics and Statistics* (November).

_____. 1990b. "New Data Bases in Human Resources: The Characteristics of Business Owners Data Base." *The Journal of Human Resources* (Fall).

_____. 1990c. "Self-Employment Trends Among Mexican Americans." Working paper. U.S. Bureau of the Census Center for Economic Studies (October).

Bates, Timothy, and William Bradford. 1977. "Loan Default Among Black Entrepreneurs Forming New Central City Business." *The Quarterly Review of Economics and Business* (Autumn).

_____. 1979. *Financing Black Economic Development*. New York: Academic Press.

Bates, Timothy, and Daniel Fusfeld. 1984. *Political Economy of the Urban Ghetto*. Carbondale: Southern Illinois University Press.

Bates, Timothy, and Caren Grown. 1992. "Commercial Bank Lending Practices and the Development of Black-Owned Construction Companies." *Journal of Urban Affairs* (Winter).

Bates, Timothy, and Donald Hester. 1977. "Analysis of the Commercial Bank Minority Lending Program: Comment." *Journal of Finance* (December).

Bates, Timothy, and Alfred Nucci. 1989. "An Analysis of Small Business Size and Rate of Discontinuance." *Journal of Small Business Management* (October).

Bearse, Peter. 1983. *An Econometric Analysis of Minority Entrepreneurship*. Washington, D.C.: U.S. Department of Commerce.

_____. 1984. "An Econometric Analysis of Black Entrepreneurship." *The Review of Black Political Economy* (Spring).

Bendick, Marc, and David Rasmussen. 1986. "Enterprise Zones and Inner City Economic Revitalization." In *Reagan and the Cities,* edited by George Peterson and Carol Lewis (Washington, D.C.: The Urban Institute).

Birch, David. 1987. *Job Creation in America*. New York: Free Press.

Boorman, John, and Myron Kwast. 1974. "The Startup Experience of Minority-Owned Commercial Banks." *Journal of Finance* (September).

Braddock, Henry, and James McPartland. 1987. "How Minorities Continue to Be Excluded from Equal Employment Opportunities: Research on Labor Market and Institutional Barriers." *Journal of Social Issues* (Spring).

Bradford, William. 1988. "Wealth, Assets, and Income of Black Households." Unpublished manuscript.

Brennan, M., and E. Schwartz. 1978. "Corporate Income Taxes, Valuation, and the Problem of Optimal Capital Structure." *The Journal of Business* (January).

Brimmer, Andrew. 1966. "Desegregation and Negro Leadership." In *Business Leadership and the Negro Crisis,* edited by Eli Ginsberg (New York: McGraw-Hill).

149

Brimmer, Andrew, and Henry Terrell. 1971. "The Economic Potential of Black Capitalism." *Public Policy* (Spring).

Browne, Robert. 1971. "Cash Flows in a Ghetto Economy." *The Review of Black Political Economy* (Spring).

Danziger, Sheldon, and Peter Gottschalk. 1986. "Unemployment Insurance and the Safety Net for the Unemployed." Discussion paper. Madison, Wis.: Institute for Research on Poverty.

Eisinger, Peter. 1984. "Black Mayors and the Politics of Racial Advancement." In *Readings in Urban Politics: Past, Present, and Future,* edited by Harlan Hahn and Charles Levine (New York: Longmans).

Evans, David. 1987. "The Relationship Between Firm Growth, Size, and Age: Estimates for 100 Manufacturing Industries." *The Journal of Industrial Economics* (June).

_____, and Boyan Jovanovic. 1989. "An Estimated Model of Entrepreneurial Choice Under Liquidity Constraints." *Journal of Political Economy* (August).

Geschwender, James. 1977. *Class, Race, and Worker Insurgency.* New York: Cambridge University Press.

Handy, John, and David Swinton. 1983. *The Determinants of the Growth of Black-Owned Businesses: A Preliminary Analysis.* Washington, D.C.: U.S. Department of Commerce.

_____. 1984. "The Determinants of the Rate of Growth of Black-Owned Businesses." *The Review of Black Political Economy,* Vol. 12 (Spring).

Harris, Candie. 1983. "Small Business and Job Generation: A Changing Economy or Differing Methodologies." Mimeo. Brookings Institution.

Harrison, Bennett, and Barry Bluestone. 1985. *The Great U-Turn: Corporate Restructuring and the Polarization of America.* New York: Basic Books.

Heckman, James, and Brook Payner. 1989. "Determining the Impact of Federal Antidiscrimination Policy on the Economic Status of Blacks." *The American Economic Review* (March).

Holmes, T., and J. Schmitz. 1990. "A Theory of Entrepreneurship and Its Applications to the Study of Business Transfers." *Journal of Political Economy* (June).

Holsey, A. 1938. "Seventy-Five Years of Negro Business." *The Crisis* (July).

Ihlanfeldt, Keith, and David Sjoquist. 1990. "Job Accessibility and Racial Differences in Youth Employment Rates." *American Economic Review* (March).

Jaynes, Gerald, and Robin Williams, eds. 1989. *A Common Destiny: Blacks and American Society.* Washington, D.C.: National Academy Press.

Jovanovic, Boyan. 1982. "Selection and Evolution in Industry." *Econometrica* (May).

Kelsey, Carl. 1903. "The Evolution of Negro Labor." *Annals of the American Academy of Political and Social Science,* Vol. 21.

Ledebur, Larry, and H. Garn. 1980. "The Role of Small Business Enterprise in Economic Development." Mimeo. Washington, D.C.: The Urban Institute.

Levinson, Daniel. 1980. "A Study of Preferential Treatment: The Evolution of Minority Business Enterprise Assistance Programs." *George Washington Law Review,* Vol. 49.

Markwalder, Donald. 1981. "The Potential for Black Business." *The Review of Black Political Economy* (Spring).

_____. 1983. "A Response to Timothy Bates' Comment." *The Review of Black Political Economy* (Winter).

Myrdal, Gunnar. 1944. *The American Dilemma.* New York: Harper and Brothers.

National Institute of Government Purchasing. 1984. "Minority Business Participation in State and Local Government." Unpublished report.

Oakland, William, Frederick Sparrow, and H.L. Stettler. 1971. "Ghetto Multipliers: A Case Study of Hough." *Journal of Regional Science* (November).

Osborne, Alfred. 1976. "The Welfare Effect of Black Capitalists on the Black Community." *The Review of Black Political Economy* (Summer).

Osborne, Alfred, and Michael Granfield. 1976. "The Potential of Black Capitalism in Perspective." *Public Policy* (Fall).

Pierce, Joseph. 1947. *Negro Business and Business Education.* New York: Harper and Brothers.

Ransom, Roger, and Richard Sutch. 1977. *One Kind of Freedom.* New York: Cambridge University Press.

Schaffer, Richard. 1973. *Income Flows in Urban Poverty Areas.* Lexington, Massachusetts: Lexington Books.

Simms, Margaret, ed. 1988. *Black Economic Progress: An Agenda for the 1990s.* Washington, D.C.: Joint Center for Political Studies.

Sternlieb, George, and Robert Burchell. 1973. *Residential Abandonment: The Tenement Landlord Revisited.* New Brunswick, New Jersey: Transaction Press.

Stevens, Richard. 1984. "Measuring Minority Business Formation and Failure." *The Review of Black Political Economy,* Vol. 12 (Spring).

Tabb, William. 1972. "Viewing Minority Economic Development as a Problem in Political Economy." *American Economic Review* (May).

_____. 1979. "What Happened to Minority Economic Development?" *The Review of Black Political Economy* (Summer).

Terrell, Henry. 1971. "Wealth Accumulation of Black and White Families." *Journal of Finance* (May).

U.S. Bureau of the Census. 1975. *Survey of Minority-Owned Business Enterprises.* Four volumes. Washington, D.C.: Government Printing Office.

_____. 1985. *1982 Survey of Minority-Owned Business Enterprises.* Four volumes. Washington, D.C.: Government Printing Office.

_____. 1987. *1982 Characteristics of Business Owners.* Washington, D.C.: Government Printing Office.

_____. 1990. *Survey of Minority-Owned Business Enterprises: Black.* Washington, D.C.: Government Printing Office.

U.S. Commission on Civil Rights. 1986. "Minority and Women Set-Aside Statement." Unpublished paper.

U.S. Comptroller General. 1973. *Limited Success of Federally Financed Minority Businesses in Three Cities.* Washington, D.C.: General Accounting Office.

_____. 1981. *The SBA 8(a) Program: A Promise Unfulfilled*. Washington, D.C.: General Accounting Office.

Vaughn, Roger. 1983. *State Tax Policy and the Development of Small and New Business*. Washington, D.C.: Coalition of Northeastern Governors.

Watkins, Linda. 1985. "Minorities' Enrollment in College Retreats After Its Surge in '70s," *Wall Street Journal* (May 29).

Joint Center Board of Governors

JOINT CENTER PUBLICATIONS OF RELATED INTEREST

Black Economic Progress: An Agenda for the 1990s, edited by Margaret C. Simms

Meeting the Croson *Standards: A Guide for Policy Makers,* by Thomas Boston

Minorities and Privatization: Economic Mobility at Risk, by Robert E. Suggs

Moving Up With Baltimore: Creating Career Ladders for Blacks in the Private Sector